"This book speaks to my heart. As a remote outpost nurse and a co-worker, I feel that this book captures the essence of the north and that of a travel nurse. I highly encourage anyone who is interested in learning more about the life of a travel nurse to remote locations, to pick up this book. I assure you; you wouldn't be able to put it down."
Nadya Aaryan-Hussain, Travel Nurse
Canadian Arctic

"A delightful read
more about nc
memory lane fc
challenge. Samy
journeys, shar
emotions. There
with her, and of cc.....

fact with her – it's all about the sex ed!"
Lisa Fréchette, BNRN, Nurse Practitioner
Nursing Student then co-worker of Samy's
in Charlottetown, Labrador (1997–1999)

"For the nurse who is seeking adventure, has a conviction to make a difference and wants to practice to one's full scope; this book is a beautiful collection of what Northern Nursing is."
Donnie Sampson, RN, MN-NP FAA
Vice president/Chief Nursing Officer 2014–2023

To,

Alex,

Enjoy.

Sammy Wilson.

AN ITINERANT NURSE

NURSE

The Ultimate Nursing Experience

Thanks and Acknowledgements

There were many people who helped me on this writing journey of mine. I am ever so grateful to so many.

Firstly, to my niece, Yogitha Jayaraman. She had faith in my endeavour.

Bryan, my other half, he was always supportive in all I do. He was there to answer my questions on the material. In fact, he prompted many forgotten memories.

To the great friends who read and supplied their input, I am forever grateful to; Margaret Tonge, Chris Tonge, Sue Marshall.

Colleagues of mine, Marilyn and Carl Kippenhuck, answered so many questions that I felt needed to be clarified. Gwendoline Wildman besides clarifying some faded memories was also instrumental in telling me about PublishU's writing course. I am thankful to her for that. Similarly, there was Andrea (her request to use only her Christian name) who also clarified some forgotten memories. Donnie Sampson read and contributed her comments. I appreciated that. Nadya Hussein's enthusiasm in my memoir gave me a boost to my writing. Lisa Frechette was also enthusiastic in my writing. I am grateful to Jason Watt, who encouraged me to write, years ago.

Puvan Mailvaganam and my niece Kavitha Ranjan helped in my navigation of the internet usage with such extreme patience. I am grateful to Puvan for going the extra mile to help me compile the manuscript to the end. Then there is Arjunt Gobinathan, my grandson, (my sister's grandson and mine as well) who helped with the front cover design.

Tony Powell, I am humbled and grateful by his contribution.

My cohort at PublishU helped with suggestions. I am pleased to have been part of an amazing group. I am looking forward to reading their books.

I am grateful to Matt Bird, for helping me navigate into the world of writing and successful publishing.

"One's knowledge is only a handful of sand. There is still an ocean of knowledge to learn."

A Tamil Proverb by Auvaiyaar.

Dedicated to the memory of my late, beloved Uncle Subramaniam S/O Krishnasamy Vandayar, without whom I would never have been able to travel to the UK to do nursing. My father's older brother was also instrumental in getting me interested in reading at a very young age.

Contents

Forward

Introduction

Foreword

A compelling read! "An Itinerant Nurse: The Ultimate Nursing Experience." It's truth to life experiences of nurse Samy. Her simplistic style of writing will certainly captivate your mind as you become entwined in her nursing journey. Her unwavering commitment to caring for the most vulnerable – our sick and especially those of us who live in the north – is compelling. Her ability to adapt to the community and communicate with her patients and provide them with compassion, care, kindness, empathy and understanding sometimes at their worst life moments, are just a few aspects of her personality. Integrity and advocacy coupled with a great sense of humour is why she was so loved by her patients. Her long nursing career is truly inspirational!

Tony F. Powell
Author, *Against the Wind – Hope sees the Invisible*

SAMY WILSON

Introduction

Retirement came unexpectedly with the pandemic in 2020 and flights and flying restrictions were in place making travelling between Cyprus and Canada a melodrama. I turned seventy at the same time. It seemed like a good time to retire.

Retirement I envisaged as being in a mildly warm sunlit rose garden; a comfortable bench to sit on with my legs up. Having my legs up is a must for comfort with books to read at leisure. "So many books, so little time," says it for me. There are plenty of roses in the garden. Besides the roses there are a guava tree, eight olive trees, a walnut tree, a mandarin orange tree, a lemon tree and a plum tree (that only bore fruits once). There is a grapevine to sit under. There are plenty of bugs to torment anyone wanting a laid-back life in Cyprus. There are mosquitoes, bees and all kinds of caterpillars. There is always some creepy crawly thing or ants dropping on you from the grapevine. There are beautiful butterflies and varied praying mantises. There are the sounds of cicadas to deafen your ears during the day and they must be able to note the time because they stop the noise from dusk on. There are a variety of birds to look at and listen to. The crows are a work of study. The interest they show in everything that goes on around them is a joy to watch. They sit on the wires and cock their heads to look so curiously.

The bee-eaters are my favourite birds to watch. They are multi-coloured birds with a distinctive call. They migrate up from Africa in the spring and again at the end of summer when they fly back to Africa. They swoop around and snatch their insects in mid-flight. It's amazing and funny to watch them thump the insect on the electric wire to get rid of the bee stingers I suppose before eating. It's a grand show right in front of the house porch. They are hardly around for more than a couple of weeks to a month. Usually, I hear them for a couple of days before I see them for a few short days.

Then there are the cats. I started feeding a cat that sat and meowed at the door. It looked half starved. Now I have about twenty-five cats to feed and at times more. Some of them are menaces. Some are so beautiful and then there are the demanding ones. Every so often a stray arrives, looking half-starved and anxious. The other cats look at it with such utter affront, "How dare you turn up here!" and they try to see it off. With not much enthusiasm, they eventually let it hang around and share their food. That's how the menagerie has swelled. Bryan says, "If you feed them, then you have the responsibility to neuter them too." Food and vet bills have spiralled out of control. One of them, Lady Jane Grey, turned up with a broken leg. The vet fixed it with a rod in the leg. She was doing fine. Six months later, the rod broke the skin at the joint and was visible. The vet took out the rod and she has been fine since.

There are sadly abandoned dogs too and especially one big brown dog, a gentle dog that comes to eat the cat food. When it comes, the cats refuse to move from the dishes and they glare at it. It barks at them from a distance and I have to come out of the house and move a dish closer for it to eat. It is skittish of me too, so I just leave it alone and let it eat.

On top of it all, there are the chickens: four of them from a farm close by. Every morning they run to eat the cat's food. They flap their wings at the cats to get them away from the dishes and peck away at each dish. They dirty the place with their droppings under the grapevine where I have the cats' dishes. The only positive thing about the chickens is they give the garden a good scratching.

The summer in Cyprus is just too hot to sit out. The tourists come for the hot weather. For Bryan and I at sunrise, it's an early morning dash to the beach to swim or walk and then indoors for the rest of the day with the curtains drawn shut. I must stop whinging and feel very grateful for the peace and tranquillity that Bryan and I have at this moment in our lives.

All these years I have been flying from Cyprus to another European country to change flights to Canada. There are no direct flights to Canada from Cyprus. Flying from a Mediterranean climate, a sub-tropical climate, to the cold Arctic weather is challenging when it comes to packing the appropriate attire. The climate in Cyprus is hot and dry in the summers and cooler in the winters. Only mildly cooler. In contrast, the Arctic has the frigid winter weather, that freezes your eyelashes and you're trying to untangle the lashes, opening eyes wide to separate the bottom lashes from the top. The hairs in the nostrils feel like there is something that needs to be picked at. The arctic cold is very dry, and the skin needs a lot of moisturisers. I did enjoy the travelling for most of the time, I must admit.

Age catches up and travelling was getting tiring. Enforced retirement didn't seem like such a bad idea at all. All things considered the decision was made and it happened with no great fanfare. I retired.

The thought of doing nothing else besides reading didn't seem right. There are dog sanctuaries and cat sanctuaries nearby and both are desperate for volunteers. I started volunteering at the cat sanctuary. It wasn't that I was a cat lover. I always considered myself a dog lover. So is Bryan, my husband. We love dogs. Initially, I did start volunteering at the dog sanctuary, but the poop smell got to me. It was too overpowering. Even though I am used to some awful smells, I just couldn't stand it. Cat sanctuary won.

Then there was an opportunity to learn Tamil online with Karky Research Foundation. I am a Tamil and speak Tamil but I don't read fluently. During my school years in the Catholic Convent, we were taught in English. Now I can read Tamil a little better. Karky Research Foundation also provide once a month "Ari Talks" – lectures on topics of interest of the day, in Tamil. I haven't missed one session yet. It also seemed like a good idea to do Greek lessons on Duolingo daily online; reaching 1,430 days as of 30 January 2024 and continuing to do at least half an hour daily. I still can't communicate in Greek with the

Cypriots though. I don't feel confident enough. English is used in most places in Cyprus, thankfully.

Since the pandemic started, I have kept myself busy but that doesn't seem to be sufficient. My niece, Yogitha, prompted me to write. She knew that I had wished to write for a long time already. With her encouragement I put pen to paper and then to the laptop. I am grateful to Yogitha and Bryan for their faith in me. Bryan was always rooting for me to do what I want and has helped me in any way that would make things easy for me. Whilst in the midst of writing, I found out from a good friend Gwen Wildman – we worked in Labrador together – regarding a writing course with PublishU. It provides a monthly start of a three-month writing course. That was heaven sent. I enrolled and found it a great help to write more constructively and effectively. The small group I was in, was a great bunch. We were able to learn and write, help each other with encouragement and constructive critiquing. At last, I felt I was getting somewhere with my writing.

I am filled with excitement and trepidation in completing this book.

SAMY WILSON

Chapter 1
1982: The Journey Begins

There may be references to clinics, nursing stations or health centres. I am categorising them as one and the same for the purpose of my writing. What I write is my memoir and not to be taken as an academic work for any purpose. Some nurses who have worked in the Canadian North may see things differently from me. To avoid any disagreement, let me reassure the reader that I feel greatly privileged and honoured in having worked in the north. There had been a great deal of pride and pleasure in being among the Inuit, First Nations people and the Métis.

One of my sincere hopes is that there will be young nurses who may be enticed by my memoir to try out nursing in the vast Arctic and Sub-Arctic. The experience is all worthwhile. The people, the landscape, the Northern Lights and the wildlife are just simply amazing.

All the narratives mentioned here are also from my own involvement. There are many incidences that I know are the experiences of other nurses and are greatly relevant as well as fascinating, but they are not mine to tell. As the saying goes, everyone has a book in them. There was never a dull moment in the north. Every day brought its own absorbing and captivating happenings. There was always something to tweak the day. It might be a polar bear sighting or a film crew in town.

As a State Registered Nurse and a State Certified Midwife in the UK, I enjoyed the experience of being a midwife in Rossendale Maternity Unit in Lancashire. After qualifying as a midwife, I married Bryan Wilson, on the 23 April 1977, Saint George's Day. We bought a lovely semi-detached house a year later; with a deposit payment, left for Bryan from his grandfather, who had died on our wedding day. We didn't know he had died till the next day. Our house overlooked a green belt area. Bryan was also a member of the Rossendale Search and Rescue Team and we had a border collie that he started to train as a search and rescue dog. We were well settled with walking distances to both our workplaces.

Working with experienced midwives, I watched and learnt a great deal on caring for women from prenatal to delivery and postnatal. I found out that it is after qualifying and not during the training that you really grasp what it is that we learnt. The maternity unit was in a beautiful setting overlooking green fields that had sheep grazing and rabbits frolicking in them. A woman in labour would have found it all very soothing. I remember the idyllic scenes and the camaraderie present in that unit. That hospital has since been torn down; in its place, houses were built as a residential area.

Into my fifth year of marriage, I started feeling restless and perused the nursing magazines and found employment postings in Canada. Of course, it didn't please Bryan. Even though it was going to be a difficult decision to part from Bryan temporarily, I went ahead and applied and was offered employment with Health and Welfare Canada. Promising Bryan to do only two years, I accepted the job offer and resigned my midwifery post.

Travel plans were made and Bryan and I travelled to London. At Heathrow, flights were cancelled due to thick fog. We were provided accommodation for the night in a hotel. Next morning, I said goodbye to Bryan and set off on the long journey to Manitoba. It was hard leaving Bryan, but I was still excited and nervously looked forward to new adventures ahead. He was excited for me but, at the same time, I knew he was sad. We knew we would be together soon for our holidays.

From Heathrow to Toronto and onwards to Winnipeg, a long journey. At the hotel that I had to check in to, in Winnipeg there were two other Canadian nurses who were also journeying to Thompson for orientation with me next day. They were new recruits like me. We shared our stories with each other. It was good to have the company to travel to our orientation.

At Thompson, where the Health and Welfare northern office in Manitoba was, we met our supervisors and other staff members. We were welcomed very warmly. The orientation was quite interesting and covered quite a lot of relevant information. For a start we learnt about the culture of the people we were going to serve. They were the

First Nations people: the Cree and Dene. Then there were the Métis and Inuit.

We did health assessment. This was a new and interesting start. It's learning to examine the whole person. We had to have our assessment all done when we consulted the community doctor on call with urgent cases. The documentation was the most important lesson and how we do that was made clear to us. Documenting on date, time and all that the patient tells you, how the patient actually looks, and what was done by the nurse. The assessment carried out by the nurse and a nurse's conclusion and plan. The documentation is there for the next nurse and or the doctor to see, what has been done thus far, if the patient isn't getting better or is worsening. Most importantly, if the same nurse sees the patient next time, she has her documentation in front of her to proceed with what needs to be done next. History of a patient is vital documentation.

We learnt about cloud formation and weather patterns. This was to help us answer the pilots' questions about the weather in our community before they have to fly into the northern community for the medical evacuation. This was the early 1980s. We came to understand then that we did our own medivacs. That was, we escorted our patient out in emergencies from the community to the city hospital. Though for most of the north, the medevac plane arrives with the medevac nurse. Before they leave their base, the medevac nurse liaises with the community nurse and if necessary, extra things like blood, which is not stocked in the northern communities, are brought in. Sometimes two nurses are needed for a patient who might be intubated.

In some northern communities the community nurse still has to do their own medevacs.

We would be learning about the day-to-day clinic work and be guided by the nursing staff already in place. It was very stimulating and exciting. I was raring to go.

There was an emergency holdall bag that was provided at the orientation. Each nurse had her own holdall. It was huge, heavy, as well as clumsy. It had a sleeping bag and a survival kit. I remember the survival kit had a fishhook. Manitoba being the land of vast number of lakes, I suppose the idea is, we could at least fish for food after a plane crash, assuming one survived the crash! It certainly was a very good idea. We also got a free, brand-new parka for use in the winter. A very warm down jacket that I used so gratefully while I was there for two years. After two years, the parka was mine. We were also encouraged to shop for our winter boots and gloves and thermal underwear in Thompson. The store had everything that one would need for living in the frigid north. We were all set to go on to our own communities. The three of us were all going to different communities.

SAMY WILSON

Chapter 2

My First Northern Community

My first despatch was to the community of Brochet. The usual schedule flight, DH Twin Otter, had been cancelled due to bad weather. It would have flown from Thompson to Lynn Lake and then on to Brochet. I soon learnt that cancelled flights due to bad weather happened frequently. Usually thick fog and blizzard conditions prevent planes flying. Amazingly, my flight into the first northern community was in a float plane – a Cessna 185. It was a chartered plane because the schedule flight wasn't flying that day. I was surprised that it was chartered just for me by the organisation. But it was the first of many flights in those small planes over the next couple of years. Especially flying to the satellite community of Tadoule Lake from Brochet, one day a week, to provide health care. There were no roads connecting the communities. That's how sometimes the northern nurses flew around with medevacs and to attend in-service trainings. Most times we travelled on scheduled flights. We called them sched flights. In that first chartered flight, the pilot flew over captivating vast landscapes of wilderness and lakes. My first sight of such vast landscapes. At one lake the pilot pointed out a moose in the lake and he swooped low over the lake, for me to see the moose clearly. It was a beautiful October autumn day with the sun shining; but a definite chill In the air. Even though I had the parka, I didn't use it then. I had on a cape and I was warm enough.

We landed on Reindeer Lake, near the community and the nurse in charge came to meet me at the dock. Andrea was from Taunton, Somerset, UK. What a small world. Andrea knew my good friend – a childhood friend from Malaysia, Leela. Leela trained and worked as a nurse in Taunton, Somerset. They knew each other well having nursed together in Taunton. I felt so much better seeing another English nurse. I had just left behind all my midwifery colleagues and I did miss them.

The community was sparsely populated, the houses were concentrated together in that vast landscape. There was hardly any traffic or sound of traffic though there were a few trucks. The roads were gravel. My first impressions were hard to describe otherwise. I was excited to have arrived for new experiences.

The community was divided into crown land and treaty land. The First Nations people, who are Cree and Dene, lived on the treaty land. It was separated by a small stream with a wooden bridge to cross over. The Métis, the Catholic mission, the school, RCMP detachment and residences, the clinic and residences, the store and people who have come from the south to work as teachers as well, lived on the crown land. People moved freely between the two communities without any restriction of any sort though.

Due to a Band Council Resolution (BCR), it was a dry community. No alcohol was allowed on treaty land. There was restlessness among some young people who objected to alcohol on the crown land. Understandably, it created some serious problems.

Residence for the nurses were in the same building as the clinic. I really liked that; though there were some trailers available that were very comfortable right in front of the clinic. When Bryan came to visit, I would move into the trailer for more privacy. It was also used by the many transients like the visiting doctors, dentists and other staff. The clinic had its own snowmobile, all-terrain vehicle (ATV) and truck. In winter the nurse on call may need to respond to an emergency and usually, depending on the weather and the terrain, one of the vehicles would be used.

It is worth mentioning that the Catholic mission had the Father, the priest, a brother who loved gardening and had a massive green house. He also loved cooking. Then there was the sister, a nun. They were French Canadians and we found them to be very hospitable. We had a few dinners at the mission.

Food from the stores was expensive. People lived off the land by hunting, trapping and fishing. Fish was plentiful in the lakes. The fish was also fed to the dogs, huskies. The huskies were used for dog teams. The people depended on their trappings of lynxes, bears, foxes, wolves to harvest their furs. The furs were cleaned and stretched out to dry. Most people use them to make their winter garments, like jackets, boots, gloves, pants and hats. Some were sold at the

Hudson Bay Store. That was their income. In the 80s there were a few snowmobiles and ATVs for travelling around. There was no year-round road. An ice road in midwinter was cleared for goods to come in the trucks. It was for a very short duration only in those days.

The RCMP detachment had two officers and they were kept well occupied, mostly with minor infringements.

The teachers were an interesting bunch of southerners. They were very committed teachers. There was an older lady teacher, originally from Poland, and her husband was a farmer with his sons in the south. He used to travel up from Winnipeg with fresh farm produce of meats and vegetables and fruits. We were invited to a few meals when he came to visit his wife. Another teacher was born in Guyana, his ancestors were from the Indian continent. It was most interesting to meet an Indian from Guyana. I didn't know there were Indians like me in Guyana.

I was in my early thirties and found it all so interesting. There was so much to take in and I was enjoying everything about life in the north.

One of the main obstacles that people faced living in the North was being reliant on flights to fly in and out due to the unpredictable weather. When nurses were waiting to go out after their work term is up and if the weather "comes down" and flights are delayed, they became stressed. Then the nurses waiting to fly into the community to start their term are delayed in the cities at airports. It becomes tedious, as I soon found out to my cost. Waiting at airports if the flights are cancelled, then to rebook on the next available flight and return to the hotel. Sometimes it might even be a few days of to-ing and fro-ing. It does get tiring. The nurse waiting to go out might miss a special occasion like a child's birthday or having to cancel flights of a booked holiday with loved ones. That was something you just learnt to put up with. There is no negotiating with nature.

SAMY WILSON

Chapter 3
Nursing in Isolation

Nursing in the north was a unique experience for me. We were the frontline health care providers for the community in an emergency and all illnesses. We were the Community Health Nurses, known as CHN, (pronounced chin). It was a three-nurse station, with no doctors on site. The doctor was on call over the phone to consult in an emergency, 120 kilometres away south. There were nurses of different specialty, and it was good in that sense that there was always someone who was an expert in one thing or another. I had midwifery experience. Another may have experience in ICU or Accident and Emergency or Paediatric nursing. We complemented each other. It reminded me somewhat of the role of a GP, general practitioner in the UK. You are a hands-on nurse and without a doubt develop a close relationship with your patients. The nurse has a duty of care to the patient, the family and in a sense, the community. This was how I saw it. The isolation of the community and the vast distances between the communities and the nearest hospital, enables the nurse to look at nursing in isolation, holistically.

There were many nurses who did short stints, contracts, like a month to three months or even shorter or longer periods. They could be agency nurses or government employees. There were permanent government employees of Health and Welfare Canada.

The support workers, like the receptionists, the clerks, maintenance man, the cleaners, and CHR, community health representative — they are really our right-hand personnel from the community. We could not do without their support, in the day-to-day running of the clinic and most certainly in emergencies. Besides being translators for their own people of Inuit and First Nations; many elderly do not speak English, they help in calming a child or an adult and helping in whatever way they can and as needed by the nurse. I was grateful for their presence and help.

There is a first nurse on call after clinic hours and a second if there are more emergencies or if the first nurse on call requires more hands to manage an emergency. Usually if that's the case there is a medevac being arranged. The nurse may have to go out with the patient on the medevac and there might be more urgent patients to be seen.

After an emergency was identified by the nurse, a consultation with the doctor on call takes place. There was a radiophone which was not at all ideal. It was always crackling. The only phone line is a party line shared by five in those days. The clinic, the RCMP, the store, school and the mission. When someone picks up the phone there is a sound that immediately alerts the others that the phone is being used. Human nature being what it is, people are curious. Confidentiality is compromised. In the 80s there was no private phone in Brochet, let alone internet. Most of the time the doctor would advise on the appropriate treatment and/or a medevac.

My first memorable medevac was a toddler, a near drowning. I was at the end of the hall in the clinic one fine morning and witnessed the scene of a man bringing in what I thought was a wet, bedraggled doll. The realisation that he had a limp child in his arms shocked us into activity. The toddler had been found outside the house in a small puddle of water, face down. We resuscitated the toddler and stabilised her before I medevacked the child out. I was not a good flyer. Throughout the journey into Lynn Lake, I was vomiting, in turns caring for the child. I remember the pilots kept looking back at me. The child recovered very well and returned to the community after a few days.

We had one satellite community further north of Brochet, called Tadoule Lake. To get to it was by a charter flight. It was a beautiful community with a good lake that I had fished out of many times when I overnighted there. The Dene people of Tadoule Lake were located from Little Duck Lake to Churchill Manitoba in 1956. That move was not ideal for the people. There were many casualties of alcohol. So, they relocated to Tadoule Lake. It had a small clinic to work out of and I had stayed many times overnight at the clinic. There was a young woman employed as a lay dispenser and a maintenance man in the community. She would call to consult us with concerns if there was anyone needing medical care. We would advise accordingly.

There was frequent changeover of nurses even in those days. Once there was a new nurse arriving on a charter and by the time the plane landed on the lake, we were waiting at the dock with a medivac to go out. The new nurse volunteered to go with the medivac. Her luggage was unloaded, and she went but did not return. She went home, deciding that northern nursing wasn't her forte. We felt bad that we put a new nurse in that position. We learnt a lesson at her expense.

Sick clinics are conducted in the mornings and some may need more tests and follow-ups. Like X-rays or blood works. We were able to dispense some medications. With protocols in place to guide nurses, we were able to treat patients effectively and safely.

Monday to Friday afternoons were the routine clinics. The well-women clinics, which included yearly pap smears for women who were also taught breast self-exam, were all part of the well-women assessment. There were guidelines to how often the pap smears were done. I don't remember well-man clinics in those days. Menopause women were vulnerable to so many uncomfortable symptoms and we were able to provide them with information to cope with their symptom. If necessary, they are listed to be seen by the visiting community doctor who might consider medication to help relieve their symptoms.

Well-child clinics would involve assessment of the child development, including weight and height and generally checking the child was growing healthily, especially in the first year. Mums' concerns were taken seriously and acted on or a welcome reassurance provided. The child was immunised – again according to the protocols of the north. A pre-school child's exam also included eye and hearing tests. A dental referral was done if the child has not been seen by a dentist yet. Pre and postnatal clinics were on another afternoon. The prenatal clinics were always attended by the women and their excited partners and their older kids so that they can get to listen to the baby's heartbeat. The chronic disease follow-ups were at intervals of three-monthly or six-monthly depending on how well they were coping with their diabetes or heart disease or lung disease and booking them for their blood tests or X-ray at regular intervals again as per protocol demanded.

The clinics were well-organised in the communities and provided very good health care to the people of the north. When we came across any case that needed to be followed up by the community doctor, then they were listed to be seen at their next visit. The community doctor did visit once a month, from Monday to Friday – weather permitting, that is. Sometimes the doctor may have to refer the patients on to a specialist – to a paediatrician if it's a child and gynaecologist/obstetrician for prenatal or anything to do with female sexuality, including menopause. For the man, he might need the urologist. Then people were referred to the internist for chronic diseases.

On Friday afternoons we stocked the cupboards and the emergency room and ordered drugs and other stock that we would be running short of. We would stock up as soon as an emergency is over and everything was checked and ready for the next emergency.

The dentist visited very regularly about four to six visits a year and was always very busy. The opticians co-ordinated their visits with the ophthalmologist. The diabetics are followed up very closely by the ophthalmologist as well. The opticians bring a good selection of spectacles. Going to the city shopping for spectacles wasn't an option. Travel by air was expensive and the only way out as there were no roads.

The mental health team did regular visits as well. It was a well-needed service. The social worker sometimes had to manage the mental health patients as well.

As nurses in remote communities, we wore different hats as the situation warranted. First, we were nurses. Then we took on roles for the different services. We learnt to do X-rays mostly of the chest or limbs – never the head or pelvis. Usually, the maintenance man was the one who did the X-rays during clinic hours. Even with training (but not as intensively as radiologists), they were not allowed to do head and pelvis X-rays. After hours, we did the X-rays if needed. We became phlebotomists and lab-technicians. A cleaner. A dental role, as sometimes we did temporary fillings. Many a patient would beg to have a painful tooth pulled out which we couldn't do. Though I have also known patients, especially young men, pulling out their own offending tooth. Many a times we had to be social workers and mental health counsellors. Sometimes we were ambulance drivers. We didn't have ambulance drivers in North Manitoba in the early 80s. We also had the task of looking after the animals in the community as well.

In Brochet, I remember, my colleague Andrea and I were pulling porcupine quills from one of the teacher's dog's muzzle. It was summer and the teachers were away, and the dogs were left to friends to be looked after. They were outdoor dogs anyway and were never tethered. We did notice this particular dog that we liked hadn't been around for a few days. Then when he did turn up one Saturday, with his best buddy, we noticed he had all these quills on his muzzle and the muzzle was festering. He was a gentle dog but a big dog like a husky. We decided to pull the quills out anyway since they were festering. He was a good dog and allowed us to pull them out. But every time we pulled one out, he would let out a loud howl and his buddy would bark at us more or less telling us to stop hurting his friend. They came out easily enough. We couldn't help laughing and it was funny. That's when we got a call from our supervisor from Thompson to inform us of a tragedy. A long-time nurse from Lac Brochet, North of Brochet, had retired and was flying out with her husky dogs in a small plane. It had blown up in the air, killing all of them. I didn't know her well, but Andrea had had conversations with her over the phone. That really sobered us. We felt so sad. The nurse was retiring and had arranged everything for the dogs as well as herself and she had died so

SAMY WILSON

tragically. To go back to the dogs, we did a fairly good job and cleaned the muzzle and started him on antibiotics, fed him, provided a bowl of water and made a comfortable place for him just outside the doorway. He laid down and that was it, we didn't see him move from there for a few days. There was nothing wrong with his legs, but he must have decided he was a sick dog and needed pampering. He ate well. His surroundings were clean. About three or four days later, early one morning, I sneaked a peak through the curtains. There he was frolicking around with his best buddy. He saw me and realised his game was up. That was so funny too. He had worked out how to get sympathy.

During the two years in Northern Manitoba, I moved around to other clinics when our own clinic was well staffed and another clinic was understaffed. This gave me the opportunity to see other northern communities in Manitoba and to work with other nurses. I felt I learnt a lot working with the different nurses and gained more experiences.

I was fortunate enough to be in God's Lake Narrows' community during a break-up. I woke up to a strange sound. I got up, dressed and went out to the river nearby and found the frozen river was breaking up and the sounds of the ice tinkling with the moving ice was an amazing sight and sound. I never forgot that sound. Just imagine a river of shard ice moving and the tinkling sound.

In one of the communities, I worked with a male Welsh nurse. I was on-call one night and a man had come in with a friend with a scalp wound. He had sustained a laceration to his scalp during an alcohol altercation. Though they were inebriated, they were polite and calm. But they kept looking at me while I was inserting sutures to the laceration. I was wondering where my colleague was, knowing that at times he would go visiting people in the community. At that very moment, he walked past my door with his dog. What a great relief it was to see him walk past, and he did greet the guys. The guys left just as quietly as they came in.

In another community I was working with two other lovely nurses whom I will never forget. One was a white Canadian but with Rastafarian hair locks and I worked with her again later on the Labrador coast. The other was a tall blonde beauty who fell in love with the RCMP in that community. They got married and had two girls and lived in eastern Canada. One night we got called to say a man was bleeding at his house and needed a nurse to see him at the house. On further questioning we learnt that he had been stabbed and the perpetrator was still at the house. We had been given strict guidelines not to do home visits after hours due to alcohol and violence going on at that time in the community. After a great deal of negotiations, the man was brought in with the help of the RCMPs. He had a small stab wound to his thigh, but he appeared to have lost a lot of blood. Intravenous fluids were pushed and after consulting with the doctor-on-call, arrangements were made and he was medevacked. In the midst of all that, a young woman came in in labour and delivered a baby with no problems. It was a busy night.

Bryan came to visit me in Brochet twice. Once in the summer and once in the winter. As promised, I returned to the UK after two years in Manitoba. That was the start of my fascination with the kind of nursing that I had experienced. I didn't merely nurse the symptom but a whole individual, the family and the community.

I walked straight back into midwifery, the place I left, as if I had never left at all. My midwifery colleagues were very interested in the Canadian northern nursing. I had been writing to a colleague with my life in the north and she had been able to share my news with the rest.

I learnt to drive and got my driving licence and became a community midwife. That kept me happy and content for a while. Working with General Practitioners (GPs) and being able to work with them in their prenatal clinics was interesting and I got to know the women. Conducting prenatal classes and getting to know the pregnant women was very useful when eventually I had to attend them during their postnatal period in their homes. At least they would know me then.

Restlessness got me again. Back over the pond I went, to Canada, Labrador this time. It would have put any husband to a severe test, but, though Bryan was not pleased, he never stopped me going. He is a man of great patience and tolerant of his restless wife. We have been married now for forty-six years.

SAMY WILSON

Chapter 4

The Big Land: Labrador

A land of unspoilt scenery. Labrador is called the "Big Land" by the Labradorians. It's a vast land with tall trees. In some parts of Labrador, in the autumn, there's a beautiful display of tree leaves changing colour to hues of reddish brown and gold on the landscape. You didn't have to go to Maine or Vermont to see the beauty of the autumn foliage, in magnificent colours. Labrador was a captivating place.

There was wildlife, like black bears, wolves, foxes, lynx, marten and beaver. The polar bears show up on ice floes in spring and summer. Ptarmigans are hunted as a delicacy. Gulls' eggs are picked. The geese and ducks fly in in the spring and fly out with their new offspring at the end of summer. People wait eagerly for the geese to fly in. They like the geese eggs and the meat.

The lakes and rivers are teeming with trout and salmon during salmon runs in the summers. There is the capelin that rolls on to spawn in the summer as well. On the North Labrador coast, the char is plentiful. I learnt to fish for the chars with hook and line whilst on the north coast. Caribou and moose are plentiful, and people love to hunt and use the skin to sew boots and jackets and gloves. The meat is frozen, bottled, canned or dried.

In the fall, there are berries to pick: blackberry, partridge berry and blueberry. The bakeapple are picked earlier. In some communities, they even get wild damsons. People are quite secretive about their berry-picking grounds. To be out in the wilderness away from the community is like getting a complete relaxation break. They do keep an eye out for the black bear though, as they to wish to eat the berries before hibernating.

At this stage it would be remiss of me if I didn't mention Doctor Wilfred Grenfell briefly, as I came to work for The Grenfell Regional Health Authority then. The Health Authority's name has since changed. Many books have been written of Doctor Grenfell and he himself wrote many books.

Doctor Wilfred Grenfell, a surgeon, came to the Labrador coast in 1892 as a missionary. He established schools, hospitals, orphanages, nursing stations and four hospital ships (besides starting fourteen industrial centres, a co-operative lumber mill and agricultural stations). He raised money from his lecture tours in Canada and the US to establish the above establishments for the fisher people of the coast of Labrador and Newfoundland. He was instrumental in the recruitment of volunteer nurses and doctors, who came to work in these areas. Sir Wilfred Grenfell was knighted by King George V in 1927 for his services to the people of Labrador and Newfoundland.

It was 1987 and I was employed to work for the Grenfell Regional Health Authority. The first posting was to Postville for a couple of months as a stop gap while waiting for a new nurse who had been employed for the post there, but she was delayed. The nurse who was leaving was a British girl from Mousehole in Cornwall. An artist as well, she was leaving to spend more time on her art. She was leaving the next day I got there. Time passed swiftly in those two months.

The community I was assigned to was Davis Inlet, where I worked with a number of nurses who came and went. It was a three-nurse station but there were only two of us at any one time. The clinic had a basement with a few rooms and the first floor reached by a few steps. It was an old wooden, clapped-out building. In front of the building was the Catholic church with a resident priest. There were also three nuns who lived in the community. The Innu People were Catholics. Here I worked briefly with the nurse from Manitoba, with the Rastafarian hair locks.

It was a busy place. It was a very beautiful community with magnificent tall trees then. I had the pleasure of working with some of the Innu people at the clinic and being able to get to know them. Since then, the community has been relocated to another place called Natuashish and the people are known as Mushuau Innu First Nation. On a home visit once in that community I came across some men building a huge wooden boat by hand. It was right in the middle of the house and half built already. There were wood shavings all over the floor. It was an amazing sight. It looked beautiful. My only regret was that I didn't go back with a camera. I loved their ingenuity. As it usually happens, after a couple of years, I decided to move around to work in the other nursing stations in Northern Labrador.

In Hopedale, an Inuit community, I had the opportunity to work with the legendary nurse, Anne McGilligot. Her parrot was famous as well. She lived and worked in Hopedale for a great number of years. Anne was a nurse with a great deal of experience and wealth of knowledge about nursing. She was well known to all the doctors and was greatly respected for her work. She did have her own house built and furnished in the community but didn't live in it but lived in the nursing station during the time I was there. I was honoured to have known and worked with her.

Makkovik was unique for the mix of the Inuit and Métis living there. People were very friendly and I enjoyed working with them. My colleague who worked with me was married to an Inuit, from Nain. We worked well together.

It was the first day in Makkovik and the nurse whom I was taking over from was leaving the next day. I was in a room near the emergency room that had the emergency entrance next to it. Any time I start in a community, I would be a little anxious and sleep is delayed. I heard a door opening and closing and I was pretty sure it was the emergency door. I waited a while thinking maybe the nurse was dealing with an emergency. When there was no other sound, I came out of the room and walked around, and all was quiet. It didn't feel right to me though.

So I went and woke up the nurse to ask her if she had a patient and she told me no and that she had been fast asleep. She was not overly pleased. I told her of hearing a door opening and closing and she looked sceptical. She realised I was perturbed and we walked together to the nurses' waiting room. I was still talking when I saw the shocked look on the nurse's face. I thought there was someone in the waiting room. I looked back and saw nothing and the nurse pointed to the carpet and there were the footprints. It had been raining and who ever came in had not removed their shoes as was customary and had left the wet, sandy clear prints of their boots on the carpet. Now we were definitely worried. We went around all the building but all looked secure and locked.

Earlier in the evening there had been a call by a young Inuit male with mental health problems. The nurse knew him and had counselled him over the phone and reassured herself he was fine. The nurse called the maintenance man and spoke to him regarding the intruder and whether it could have been the troubled young man. The maintenance man said that it couldn't have been the young man since that young man had been with him all evening since his call to the nurse. That really bothered us and we thought, "Who else could it have been?"

The maintenance man came in with a young man to check the building and to reassure us that it was all safe and all locked up. I asked if the young man may have left the maintenance man for a few minutes at all. The young man he was with, spoke up and said no he was with the maintenance the whole time. That was embarrassing as well, and, in a way, funny. The young mental health patient had his wits about him and was so pleasant. So that was it, we went to bed with no further mishaps that night. We never knew who the intruder was or why the intruder came that night.

The northern most community was Nain, an Inuit community and the people were Moravians. The Labrador Inuit were Moravians. The Moravian missionaries who had a huge impact on the life of the Inuit were the first Europeans to settle in Labrador. There are many books written on the arrival of the Moravian missionaries, as well as on the decimation of the Okak and Hebron population during the Influenza Epidemic of 1918 and 1919.

The Northern Inuit communities had their fair share of troubles like the Spanish Influenza epidemic in 1918 which killed two thirds of the Inuit population when they lived further north of Nain. It was a memorable time for me working in the northern most community of Labrador.

In 1992, after five years on the North Labrador coast, I moved to the south coast to Port Hope Simpson working first with Christopher Ryan and then with Gwen Wildman and Carole Wood. The nursing station was surrounded by open grounds, which had plenty of Iris growing in the summer. The ground was almost boggy. We had watched a helicopter land in the front of the nursing station one day and saw the tyres sink into the bog and the propellor got stuck in the bog too. That was that for the helicopter until a helicopter mechanic came and mended whatever needed mending before it took off again after a few days.

Our supervisor at that time was Margaret Mahood, another legend of the Grenfell Health Authority and she was based in St. Anthony on the northern peninsula of Newfoundland. Margaret Mahood was the last nurse to have travelled by dog team to the community clinics. She was always accompanied by the station driver from Rexon's Cove, Uncle Len Russell as she affectionately calls him. My memories of her were how well thought of she was on the coast of Labrador. People knew Margaret Mahood well and had great respect for her. She was a caring supervisor and looked out for us nurses.

We were also providing service to a satellite community, William's Harbour. It had a very small population. It did have a school with one teacher, Maurice Smith. Lorraine Russell was the lay dispenser and we held clinics at Lorraine's house. Lorraine lived with her father and her uncle who were lovely gentlemen. Gwen Wildman, Carole Wood, Moira Bailey and I with Bryan, attended the wedding of Lorraine and Maurice in William's Harbour, 20 August. The honeymooners were off to a cabin that night and Bryan and I slept in their bed. Gwen, Carole and Moira, the public health nurse, slept in the lounge. We had come by boat driven by Donald Sampson, the maintenance man, but returned next day by Tony Powell's charter from Charlottetown. It was a lovely memorable wedding.

Travel to William's Harbour was by boat in the summer and in winter by snowmobile. When travelling to the satellite communities, we were always accompanied by the nursing station's maintenance man. In Port Hope Simpson, it was Donald Sampson. The maintenance men were always the local people who knew the terrain well and grew up knowing the land and sea. Especially during freeze-up and break-up of ice, they are knowledgeable about the ice conditions on the lakes. Many accidents have occurred as a result of poor ice conditions. The loss of snowmobiles or even the loss of lives are rare but occur more than necessary, due to poor judgement in some cases.

Alcohol was not an item that was sold in the communities of Labrador up to the early 90s (except in the straits which was the southern part of the Labrador coast). One of the stores in Port Hope Simpson was bringing in beer for the first time, to sell in the community, legally. There was a lot of mixed reactions from the people of the community. The older people were concerned about how it might affect their young people. Many of the younger generation wanted a choice of being able to get alcohol in their community. There was a lot of buzz about it for days before the arrival of the cargo boat. With the arrival of the boat, my colleague and I went down to the dock to see how the unloading of the offending shipment panned out. It seemed like the whole population of the community had showed up for the occasion. With a lot of attempts from the elders to stop the unloading, eventually it was done and the trucks loaded. Again, the elders tried to stop the truck from leaving the dock. The shop owner did have a valid licence for his shipment, but he was very patient and respectful of the elders and took his time and managed to get it all to his shop finally. There were no arguments or other unpleasantness and it all ended amicably even though there were tense moments. The store did a good trade. Soon the other stores were bringing in beer as well.

It isn't that people didn't drink alcohol. The younger adults and the youth were the consumers. The argument was that, if there were no outlet for alcohol then less alcohol is consumed and less accidents. Drinking and driving in whatever mode isn't acceptable by any means.

Before leaving Port Hope Simpson, I must add that, that community produced a great aspiring nurse, Donnie Sampson. Daughter of Betty and Donald Sampson, Donnie returned to Labrador after her nurse training. As a northern nurse, she went on to complete her Nurse Practitioner. After that she occupied various leadership roles in the region. Donnie was a Vice President/Chief Nursing Officer from 2014–2023 for Labrador Grenfell Region. I had the pleasure of working with Donnie for a short while.

SAMY WILSON

Chapter 5
Charlottetown: Labrador

Then I moved to Charlottetown – my favourite place. It is north of Port Hope Simpson. This was the only place in which I ever spent so much time in my life: 14 years. I didn't even spend that length of time in my birthplace. That's when Bryan decided to take early retirement and moved to Charlottetown with me. We had a great life in Charlottetown. Charlottetown is the capital of Prince Edward Island in Canada. There is a Charlottetown in Newfoundland and then there is Charlottetown in Labrador.

There were two of us nurses for most of the time. Marilyn Kippenhuck was the nurse from Port Au Basque. She married a young man from the community, Carl Kippenhuck who was the maintenance man for the nursing station. Marilyn was the community nurse there a long time even before I started there. They raised their three children whilst working at the nursing station. We still keep in touch to this day. The advent of WhatsApp and Messenger have all helped to keep friendships going as strong as ever.

We had a public health nurse who did the well babies and their immunisations. More time would be spent on mother and baby and any concerns could be dealt with in a timely manner. The public health nurse would also take on some after-hours' calls and weekends which gave us good breaks to be galivanting off to the woods to cut wood in winter and relax. Lisa Frechette was one truly amazing young public health nurse. She was always looking for ways to help the young people; especially when it came to sex education, which was not addressed freely otherwise. People did find her ways unexpectedly different, but they still liked her and accepted her as a great nurse. The other public health nurse was Trina Decker. She was kind and a wonderful nurse who worked with Marilyn and I so well together. Public health nurses are a great asset in promoting healthy lifestyles and prevention of diseases. I loved what they did. Our roles overlapped in so many ways. We valued each other's role.

Charlottetown in Labrador was founded by Uncle Ben Powell, an author of numerous books, in 1950 in St. Michaels Bay. A sheltered inlet. He wanted a permanent base as a community for children to go to school and a church for people to worship. He wanted a place for people to live in all year round. Families moved in to create a community that thrived. People in Charlottetown have British ancestry as well as from the indigenous people of Labrador. They wear the mantle of Métis proudly. It has an airstrip for a plane to land. Nearly all the communities have an airstrip except Norman Bay and Pinsent's Arm. Helicopters are used usually as needed for the satellite communities.

In Charlottetown there is the Gospel Hall. There was a Pentecostal Church, which had the larger worshippers. The Anglican church was a smaller church with a smaller group of churchgoing Anglicans. One Catholic, Ida Powell, prayed at home and would have the priest at her house when he was doing his rounds. Of course, when there are weddings or christenings or funerals, people attended whichever church it was in. I was always invited when a new minister was in town and special services were held. I attended all the weddings and funerals at the different churches as it happened. The unique thing about the Gospel Hall and the Pentecostal Church was that people dressed up to go to church complete with their Sunday hats on. I found out each lady had quite a number of hats. I loved seeing them with their hats on.

Many a Sunday meal Bryan and I have had with Uncle Ben and Marie Powell. They are the most generous people we knew. There were so many people to mention who were very generous and hospitable towards us. Like the Stones, the Kippenhucks, the Turnbulls and the Powells. We had so many Sunday dinners in many different people's houses. Bryan and I loved their Sunday dinners and never turned one down! There was always a roast with salt pork and the trimmings. We loved the salt pork.

Bryan and I got ourselves two snowmobiles to use in the long winters. We had great fun riding those machines to visit our neighbouring communities or just go riding with the people of the community. We went for "boil-ups" – that's picnics – out on the land in winter. Usually, people are ice fishing on lakes for trout and they start a fire from boughs cut near the lake edge and the komatik would be turned bottom up to put out all the good food brought from home. There was a billy can over the fire to make tea.

There was homemade bread and baked cakes and pies; fresh bread eaten with bakeapple jam or partridgeberry jam. In fact, fresh bread with just the bakeapple is simply delicious. I love the partridgeberry cakes. There was smoked fish from the summer, trout, salmon and capelin. Or the fresh fish was caught right there and then and cooked over the fire. People shared their food when out on the land. The food is all homemade.

Once that's over, the komatik was straightened up and serious wood cutting was done. Bryan bought himself a chain saw and learnt how to use it and he loved cutting the wood for our furnace. He went out at first with Carl Kippenhuck who showed him areas where wood is cut: pine, birch and spruce and how to cut a tree down. He learnt a lot by watching the men. Then over the years we went by ourselves. We didn't have to be cutting long when someone going past would stop and before we knew it, they would have the trees cut and small-sized logs cut and stacked into the komatiks. I had a smaller komatik to haul as well. It was an amazing time.

That was how good people were to us in Labrador. We would come home and find a bottle of partridgeberry jam or bakeapple. Fresh bread. Smoked fish. Bottled beetroot. Or a box of frozen shrimp from Ross Turnbull who used to work on the shrimp factory ships. Ross died sadly at an early age.

Bryan would go for long walks with the dog, Cuddles, who we got unexpectedly from the family of a Pentecostal pastor. They were leaving to start their life in Newfoundland. Their new home was near a busy road and they were worried he might get onto the road and get hurt, so we took him on. Cuddles and Benji, Marilyn and Carl's dog, were the best of pals. Bryan would be seen walking with both the dogs on fine days when I was at work. Sometimes Cuddles would be alone and he would get threatened by a dog and somehow Benji would sense it and he would be there in a flash, protecting his pal. Then Cuddles would be brave with his saviour beside him and both canines would see the attacker off with its tail between its leg. Benji was known as the bear hunter. He could sniff a bear out fast. When we went to cut logs, we would take Cuddles with us. He would be running at the start of our journey and then Bryan would take him up in front of him on the snowmobile. He loved that. Sometimes, Benji would follow as well and then they both rode in the snowmobile with us. When they were running at times, they would take off into the woods and we had to wait for them to return. They were obedient, they came when Bryan whistled for them.

Most people were related to each other. There was a lot of caring and they looked out for one another. There might be some personal problems that may go well back, but when one of the community members was in need, there was no holding back. They came together in times of trouble. Similarly, with their surrounding neighbours. When someone is building a house or a shed, the men are there helping one another. People built their own houses. Big, beautiful houses. They have cabins dotted all over the place to make fishing, hunting, trapping accessible. I am speaking of the people of Charlottetown only as I was not familiar with the rest of the Labradorians' cabin life. The cabins, whether they were small or big, were luxurious homes away from home.

It is heartwarming to see the community in action. During times of illness in a family, people rally around. Logs are miraculously stacked up for their winters. Food is dropped at the house. Money is raised if their income is compromised. People work hard for their livelihood in the north.

One early morning there was a house fire, the family managed to get out, but the fire gutted the house. By mid-morning there was a meeting of the menfolk and they were out cutting logs which were hauled to the sawmills in the town. I believe there were about five sawmills. Within a few days there was sufficient planks on the site to rebuild. The women folk had a gathering that night and many items were collected for the house. It was very heartwarming to see such an outpouring of support from within the community, including from the neighbouring communities from which there were many contributions for the family.

When my arrival was new in Charlottetown; on a stormy spring day my colleague, Marilyn, phoned me to let me know that some young men from Port Hope Simpson had gone over to Norman Bay to attend the sports day and they were supposed to be heading back to Port Hope but had not arrived. The stormy weather had worsened. Visibility was nil and the storm was howling outside. My accommodation was at the health centre as well then and when I looked out, I couldn't see anything either. It was a white out. Funnily enough, due to the blowing snow, I remember it didn't exactly look dark either. I went to bed wondering when it was all going to clear and when the searchers would be going out.

The sounds of snowmobiles at the front of the clinic woke me in the early hours. I looked out to see numerous snowmobiles coming into the clinic front with bright lights on. I had gone to bed dressed appropriately for such an occasion. I ran to open the door and the rescue workers carried in two young men who I realised were alert. And two others walked in. The rescuers got down to work on getting their boots off. They cut the boots off the two young fellows they carried in. There was a thick layer of ice in their boots under their feet. I had blankets ready and put some in the dryer to warm up and used some to cover them. In fact, Marilyn and I didn't have to call for help. The men were doing everything to get the young men warmed up. Women were showing up with hot soups and hot water bottles and more blankets. The family of the lost boys had been frantic with worry, and they had been in contact by phone with the Charlottetown's folk. Charlottetown was between the communities of Norman Bay and Port Hope Simpson. It was reasonable to expect that the missing snowmobilers would be somewhere closer to Charlottetown.

The men had kept a close eye on the weather and as soon as it eased, they had set out on their snowmobiles. I didn't notice any change in the weather. The rescuers had at first found a couple of the young men in the cabin that was built by the community for such occasions. The young men had been able to start a fire in the cabin. The storm had caught them out and the melting soft snow, had got into their boots. They went searching for the rest of the group and found them. The rescuers got them to the cabin. They gave them hot sweet drinks and fed them chocolates to energise them. They returned with their young men, well-relieved to have found them safe. The family were notified by the rescuers. All checks on the young men were satisfactory besides some of their toes changed a darker colour after a few hours. All the while I was also in contact with the district medical officer regarding the young men. Besides dressing the toes and pain medication they were eventually medevacked out when the weather cleared after a couple of days and eventually back to their community. The families from Port Hope Simpson did arrive to see their young once it was travelling weather on snowmobile but not flying weather for a few more hours.

The way the people of Charlottetown went way out for one another was the way of the north in general. You looked out for one another. It could be you the next time help was needed.

There were no roads in southern Labrador until 2002 and it was still a gravel road then. It was well used. We bought a car, a Toyota Rav4. The car was pretty well-used. We made a few trips up and down that gravel road. From Charlottetown, Labrador to Blanc Sablon on Route 510, got the ferry to cross the Strait of Belle Isle and continue down Newfoundland to St Johns. From there we flew out of Canada to other parts of the world. The car would be left at the hotel we had stayed in and there had never been a problem with that car. People felt free that they could go out for a drive to other neighbourhood communities, instead of flying or by boats in the summer. In the winters, driving down or up by snowmobile was still desirable. It was fun snowmobiling.

Norman Bay and Pinsent's Arm were two satellite communities of Charlottetown. Until the road was built into Pinsent's Arm, the travel mode was by boat in the summer and snowmobile in the winter. The journey took us about thirty to thirty-five minutes each way. Aunt Mildred Campbell was the lay dispenser in Pinsent's Arm for years. Aunt Mildred and Uncle Stanley were just simply wonderful and generous-hearted people. We had their generosity of many lunches over the years. Bryan and I would never forget their kindness. We would see patients in their living room. Most people travelled to Charlottetown if they wanted to be seen.

Similarly, Norman Bay was accessed by boat in the summer and snowmobile in the winter. The lay dispenser was Violet Roberts then. Break-up and freeze-up were interesting rides. We took different routes at those times. Those were very scenic routes and we enjoyed travelling between these two communities. Carl Kippenhuck, the maintenance man, always took us to the satellite communities. Norman Bay people reminded me of the people from the south of England in the way they spoke. We met some of the kindest and friendliest people there.

Chapter 6

Charlottetown: A Polar Bear Visits

A polar came into town one day. Most days when I woke, I would dress quickly and take the dog out for a walk up to the airstrip which was about ten minutes' slow walk. This day the dog just wouldn't budge and just kept sniffing the air. I started walking up to the airstrip. The road sort of tilts up at an incline. The dog came very reluctantly and was way behind me.

I walked up to the airstrip and came down and the dog was way up in front on the return journey and got into the house without a fuss. The phone was ringing when I got in and it was Marilyn, my colleague, saying that there is a polar bear in town and it was heading towards their place. Marilyn's house was only about two minutes' walk at the back of the house.

I shouted to Bryan that there is a polar bear near Marilyn's house and I grabbed the binoculars which are always to hand and I was out of the door making sure the dog was closed in the house. I walked down the road thinking it was awfully quiet with no one out.

As I was nearing Marilyn's, she opened the front door and called me to get in quickly as the bear was heading towards me and I looked again and saw this huge animal coming towards me and I quickly got in and, all the while, I was looking back at this magnificent animal which was walking on the road by now and heading up to the airstrip. I swear the bear was looking at me too.

Then there was a sudden start of a car engine and like a flash the animal took off across the road opposite to where we were. We all came out of the house to look but not a sign of that bear. It had taken off into the woods. Then Bryan strolls down that road and when I asked him if he saw the bear, he hadn't! The road within minutes was chock-a-block with trucks loaded with guns. Then they tracked the footprints of the polar bear. It had come down from the airstrip; stood up at the window of Carl and Marilyn's house and that had set Benji off barking frantically in the house, wandered around the community and was heading up again.

There were tracks of the polar bear at the window. The polar bears usually come down on packed ice, ice floes and icebergs from the north and many are seen quite frequently in the communities and, more usually, at the cabins where they do break into. The realisation that I didn't have my wits about me that day struck home. Nobody goes out when a polar is around. No one in the community did except the thoughtless nurse! Poor Cuddles knew.

Once I did a medevac with Tony Powell from Charlottetown to St. Anthony on the northern peninsula of Newfoundland. I had delivered the patient to the nurse who would be taking the patient to the hospital which was about fifty-five kilometres away by ambulance. We were taking off when Tony casually asked if I had seen the polar bear outside the airport building. I hadn't. I knew that a polar bear in St. Anthony had a tooth extracted by the dentist there and it was recovering well and was waiting to be airlifted back to the North. I was very disappointed that I had missed a great opportunity of seeing a polar bear close up. I had to reassure myself that at least I had seen a polar bear in its free wild state.

Black bears are a common sight in the communities, usually at the dump sites. As usual someone had phoned to say that there was a black bear on the access road which leads out of Charlottetown. So, Bryan and I jumped on board with Marilyn and Carl and headed to the access road. We saw the black bear heading towards us. Seeing us, it turned around and walked away from us and Carl drove slowly, trying not to spook it but it didn't like us following and picked up speed and it was running straight towards a walker, coming towards us. The bear seeing the walker then just veered off to the side of the gravel road, into the trees. Poor man he was quite taken aback to see a black bear heading towards him. The poor black bear had a fright too, I bet.

Foxes are in abundance and they are trapped for their furs. Porcupines' quills are used in craft work. Moose in south Labrador are seen on the land. Caribou seems to be further north or on the island of Newfoundland. People go hunting during the season as and when allowed. Hunting seasons are controlled.

There was some sort of a celebration at the sports centre in Charlottetown and being on-call, I was there for a short while. The sports centre was just a few minutes' walk from the house. I opened the door of the sports centre and saw the fox in the light from the open doorway. I was nervous but thought the fox would probably be more afraid of me, so I decided to carry on walking home. And I knew that fox was following me. I couldn't see it but felt it. I kept talking to it and told it not to bite my legs. I got home and made sure our dog was kept in, Bryan and I stepped out and sure enough the fox was outside sitting on its haunches and looking up at us. We were up on a higher level looking down at it. We spoke to it, admiring it. Then people and trucks started on the road from the sports centre and the fox disappeared.

Bryan and I were delayed once in Churchill, Manitoba, by bad weather and we had booked into a hotel for the night and we were having a relaxing supper that night. It was a winter's night. A beautiful white fox trotted into our view. It stopped and looked at us and we were enthralled with that wildlife sight and it made the night that bit more magical. This was when I was working in Nunavut.

The wildlife was on our doorstep in the north. We have since felt grateful and humbled by our experiences there.

Fishing was the main livelihood of the people on the coast for five hundred years. Cod fishing. Then the Cod Moratorium of 1992 was put in place by the federal government of Canada due to the depleting cod stock. Many sold their fishing boats and fishing gear. Some took to fishing for other species. Many took to shrimp fishing and some dragged for scallops. A shrimp processing plant was built in Charlottetown, Labrador, and this brought the shrimp boats in and gave the people of Charlottetown and surrounding communities employment for the fishing season. Before the Moratorium the young people went into fishing after they left school. With the Moratorium it was very interesting to see how people were able to adapt and the school leavers went away to colleges and universities and trade schools to get into the varied professions. Looking back, I saw the youngsters doing so well. Some went away to become lawyers, doctor, pharmacists and, especially, nurses. They did amazingly well under the circumstances.

People could fish for salmon and trout during the season for their consumption but were given a quota for each household. Tags were issued for the salmon. If you were a transient like me who was living in the community, I had a smaller quota if I wanted to put a net out. I was given a net by Uncle John Kippenhuck and I was able to set the net with the help of Carl Kippenhuck, his son, who was also the clinic maintenance man. The older people are always addressed as "aunt" or "uncle" so and so. When the salmon ran, a very short season it was, we went early, about five in the morning, and set up our nets and in the evening, we went to check the nets after clinic. We had to stop if we reached our quota and our tags used. I loved fishing for our meals. Cod also could be fished for consumption but with a rod.

Uncle Paul Kippenhuck, the twin brother of Uncle John Kippenhuck used to build wooden boats. He was such a skilled worker. He used to do that in front of the clinic, which faced the bay, on the wharf he built as well. Every now and then I would run down to see his amazing work in progress. Uncle John Kippenhuck made unique furniture from scratch. All he had to do was see a diagram of a furniture and he would have made it. People learnt their craft from their elders and it's passed down.

Whilst still in Labrador, in December 2004, there was the Tsunami of the Indian Ocean. Watching the suffering of the people in Indonesia where they spoke Malay and in Sri Lanka where there were pockets of people speaking in Tamil, I understood the languages. I was born and bred in Malaysia but of Hindu religion and speak Tamil. Listening to them, I wanted to be there to help them. Speaking to different people, I realised that there were many groups getting organised to go out to Sri Lanka. The opportunity to join a group presented itself in February 2005 to travel with the Tamil doctors of Ontario-Sri Lanka.

When the people of Charlottetown knew I was going to Sri Lanka, they gave money so generously. Very young children raised money by putting on a play and inviting their family and friends. Schoolchildren raised money by getting their mums to do cold plates to sell. I was so overwhelmed with the generosity of the people. I came away from that experience with the knowledge of how swiftly anything can happen. At the same time how generous and kind people were. That nature was a force to reckon with. I was able to donate all the money that I was given to the people of Sri Lanka; especially to a village school where I was able to buy all the schoolchildren school shoes. Some of the children weren't wearing shoes to school. Even the teachers very reluctantly and shyly requested shoes. I bought footballs and cricket bats for the school. Whatever and however I helped was mitigated by the donations of the people of Charlottetown, Labrador.

It was an experience I will never forget. The devastation that nature wrought was horrendous. I saw more on television than in Sri Lanka. But what little I saw and heard from the people in Sri Lanka, was terribly sad. People were very grateful to the many international charitable organisations. I saw their relief, belief and trust in humanity.

The charitable organisations, the NGOs, were doing so many different things to try and restore some order to the people's lives. Wells were drained of the salt water and the debris brought in by the tsunami waves. Boats were given to the fishermen who lost their boats. Houses were being built. I met a lady one day whilst I was out for a walk on the beach. She struck up a friendly conversation and I found out even though she was a Sri Lankan, she lived in

Europe and when she was coming over to help financially, she said she received money from many of her friends and one of her friends came with her. They were driving around the coast that was badly affected and were giving out cash to a trustworthy person in each community to hand out to people they knew were badly in need of assistance. I thought that was amazing. All the Tamil doctors knew who she was. She was a very rich person in her own right I believe. That was such a pleasurable encounter.

The only thing that was more than memorable that stood out for me in Sri Lanka was the bullet scars on buildings: the remnants of Sri Lanka's civil war that raged from 1983 to 2009. It was an eerie feeling for me to see such a sight. It was practically everywhere. Then there were the checkpoints, manned at every junction by soldiers.

Before leaving the subject of Charlottetown, I would like to mention the pilots of Charlottetown. They are the Powell Brothers. There is Lester Powell, a legend of the Labrador coast. I have flown with Lester many times on Labrador Airways. Including medevacs. Then there is Tony Powell who did his own chartered flights out of Charlottetown. I have flown many a flight with Tony on many medevacs. Tony was diagnosed with throat cancer stage four, in 2004. He survived surgery, radiation and a long road to recovery. But he did it. In April 2005, he raced in The Marble Mountain, Race on Rock, a Newfoundland Snowmobile Race and was crowned, 'The King of The Hill.' Bryan and I were so happy when we heard that. I called Dr. O'Keefe, our community doctor, and shared the fantastic news with her. She was so happy for Tony. Benny Powell is the youngest commercial pilot in the family and also flew Labrador Airways. He is a great narrator of stories and poems of Labrador, just like his father, Uncle Ben. Another brother, Ramsey Powell, was also a pilot but was sadly killed during a flight in Mary's Harbour. I never had the pleasure of knowing Ramsey. Irving Powell the youngest in the family is a private pilot. There is a female pilot from Charlottetown as well working as a commercial pilot.

There are quite a few helicopter pilots, including a young woman from Charlottetown.

Charlottetown, Labrador, and its people, without exaggeration, will always remain my most favoured place in the world. In fact, for both Bryan and me.

Bryan and I had some serious discussion about retiring to Cyprus where we had some years back purchased a plot of land. We wanted to build a house on that plot. We set ourselves a date – 2006 – to finish up in Charlottetown. It was with heavy hearts we left. We loved the people and our life in Charlottetown. All good things come to an end.

We went to Cyprus and Bryan organised getting a small house built for the elderly us. I thought I would head up to Nunavut for a couple of years' stint. Leela who had worked in Labrador was in Nunavut. Leela and I had been childhood friends, and we did our training in the UK.

Then Leela went onto Australia and worked there for many years. When I was in Labrador she decided to try working in Labrador. She loved it. Then she went on to Nunavut. So, I went to work with her for a few weeks and I liked it. So, I decided to work in Nunavut. Instead of two years, I worked nearly fourteen years. As a short-term contract nurse, I travelled back and forth from Cyprus to Nunavut, working in different communities for different lengths of time. I accrued quite a mileage over the years. The Covid pandemic happened and I turned seventy in 2020. It seemed the right time to stop my travels to Nunavut. With all the restrictions, it did seem sensible to call it a day.

Chapter 7
Nunavut: 2006–2020

The plan was to work two years in Nunavut and then to settle down with Bryan in Cyprus. But the north lured me in and I ended up working in the various communities in the arctic and sub-arctic for fourteen years. It was an amazingly memorable time. There was a lot of travelling by air. Over those years I was flying between Cyprus and Nunavut about three or four times a year. There was always a change over at a European airport, as there were no direct flights to Canada. Flying within Canada itself was also time consuming. It came to a stage when you see the same security people and pilots and air hostesses, and they recognise you as well. The hotels near the airports came to know you as a frequent flyer and a favoured guest. The passengers are people you recognise from the different communities who greet you like long lost old friends. It's a vast country with a very small population and all those empty expansive spaces between communities, especially in the north.

Nunavut, meaning "Our Land" to the Inuit, has its pristine landscape and scrubby vegetation. The Tundra vegetation with its lichens, moss and in the summers, there are colourful flowering plants. The caribou thrives in these environments when they migrate over this landscape, they have their food growing. The geese fly in, in spring. I have seen them fly in and they stand there exhausted for a while, with heads drooping and then settle down to rest and then only after a while start eating. You could almost palpate their tiredness and their relief that they had made it. It amazes me that they do this year in and year out. Canada geese are known to fly, weather permitting 1,500 miles in a 24-hour period, to eventually get to their birthplace in the north of Canada. I have stood and watched them enthralled at their majestic flying in a V-formation. They fly south for the winter. Nature does a wonderful job in its creation.

The ravens are there in the winter but come spring, they move on; I am not sure where to and the gulls appear. The snowy owl stays all year round. The arctic foxes are ever present. The polar bears are sighted usually at the edge of town and mostly near the water, the sea. The polar bears really want the fish and the seals. I have had the pleasure of many sights of the polar bears in Nunavut. Some friendly soul in the community will phone to say that a polar bear has been sighted and does any of the nurses want to see it. If we can manage and if we are not very busy, then one or two nurses will go out with the caller to see the polar bear. At times when we are lucky we see caribou feeding behind the clinic in Coral Harbour in the summer. A captivating sight. Coral Harbour is the only community on Southampton island on the Hudson Bay with a population of just over a thousand people and is three times bigger than Cyprus, which has a population of over a million people. There are arctic hares and ptarmigans. I have seen the arctic hares in the dead of winter still able to find some blades of grass sticking out in the snow. I have seen them in Chesterfield Inlet and Coral Harbour.

The char and trout run with the spring and summer thaw. People love to fish then. When you are standing in a river, the water is teeming with fish swimming up to their spawning grounds. It's nature at its most magnificent undertaking!

The Northern Lights or aurora borealis are absolutely enchanting to watch on many a winter night. The cold nights are long in winter. Then you have the 24 hours of daylight in the summer. In the summer the children are out playing long hours because of the daylight and school is out.

Working in the north meant most of the time meeting new challenges but being guided by the protocols that were in place. Protocols are continuously updated to ensure safe practices. The guidelines are always available for most eventualities, for the nurses to refer to. They are well used. How a nurse uses it sometimes in any given situation is a different matter.

In the north I have come across so many people doing various things. They are people from various parts of the world who have settled in Canada. They do some very interesting jobs; mostly researching on a number of things relating to the Inuit people.

Once I met a researcher in Nunavut, looking at suicides in the north. Talking to her I discovered that she had done similar research in India, Tamil Nadu.

My ancestors were from that area. She said suicide was common among the elderly and they usually jump into the well. They didn't want to be a nuisance to their children in their old age. I was quite shocked to hear that. I always believed that as Indians we took care of our elders. That young woman created a dent in my perception of my culture. I don't see why it couldn't be true. We are all humans with human fallibility, never mind who and where we come from.

Chapter 8
Wearing Different Hats

As in all the northern nursing whether it be Northern Manitoba, Labrador or Nunavut where I worked, as I mentioned earlier, we wore so many hats.

We learnt to look at the X-rays we did and read them (though I can't say I mastered that skill unless it was an obvious fracture). The X-rays were sent off to be read by radiologists and we waited for the reports. If there was an urgent need to know the result, we took a picture of the X-ray and sent it to the doctor on call for further advice. In fact, in some communities the X-ray is sent electronically with the new
X-ray machines that they have as soon as it is done. Drawing blood from the most difficult of veins became an art. There was a lot to learn about drawing blood in different-coloured tops for the various tests. Some had to be sent with the blood smears on a slide. Some had serum separated and frozen prior to sending it all off.

All the nursing stations had basic laboratory equipment. To check haemoglobin, there was a haemoglobinometer. This was a basic useful tool that can show you if someone has a low haemoglobin, a sign of anaemia of some sort. It came in handy many times. There was a teenager whose haemoglobin dropped very low. Though he had been investigated over the years by a specialist in the city. He would be on iron pills but being a teenager, he would stop taking them and would not take his parents' advice. A simple non-specific test, erythrocyte sedimentation rate to measure inflammation, infection was also available. There was a microscope that was interesting to use but a challenge for me. Most doctors used them when they wanted a quick baseline for a diagnosis when they're in the community. They are simple tools and by no means gave a complete diagnosis. It is a start under the circumstances of flight delays and to work out how ill a person is. We obtained swabs from infected wounds, boils, throats, genitals. Smears and pap smears. We learnt the correct method of obtaining them so that the lab-technician would be able to carry out their work analysing them. It was disheartening to read that the swab material obtained was inadequate and the test was not done. That happened more times than I care to remember.

There are frustrating moments with the laboratory work. Due to bad weather, there might be flight delays; some lab specimens would be considered too old. In the interim while waiting for a swab result or a blood result, the patient is treated. If an antibiotic had been started and the result comes back identifying the infecting bacteria; it identifies the antibiotics that are resistant or susceptible to the infection. I loved learning all these over the years. I am a slow but ardent learner.

We were counsellors, for social work and mental health. There are social workers in most communities who work well together with the nurses in the community. Most of the time they also do counselling for the mental health patients besides the many roles they have to undertake in the northern communities. When there are no social workers in the interim, then the nurse deals with whatever needs to be done. Again, the protocols are there to guide us.

Sometimes in emergencies, we attend patients at homes or on the land. There were no ambulances in the isolated communities. We metamorphose into an emergency nurse as well as an ambulance driver as needed. During clinic hours we would have the maintenance man to drive us to the site or house. After hours we may not be able to contact the maintenance man as he may be out on the land himself, but he will respond, if he is around when called out. Usually there are plans of the layout of the community at the clinic and so making it easier to get to the emergency site in record time. Or someone from the family will be waiting to show you the way. In later years there were ambulance services started in South Labrador. A greatly needed service.

TB nurses were employed just to do the TB nursing in later years. Somehow TB is always lurking around waiting to rear its ugly head. When a new TB diagnosis was made, there was plenty of work for the TB nurse to keep her busy. Contacts must be traced and screened, and appointments made for X-rays and bloodwork and sputum collection. Sometimes there are no TB nurses available, and it falls on the nurses to do what needs doing.

In some bigger communities there were Home Care Nurses. Sometimes the nurse at the clinic carries out duties of a home care nurse when there is no home care nurse. I loved doing home visits. You get to know the people well along with their needs. These were palliative care patients mostly, being cared for in their own home. I found it rewarding to be able to help in this way.

We were pharmacists, refilling medications for patients with heart disease and diabetes and chronic illnesses and during acute infections to name a few in the interim. Usually, the prescriptions are sent off to the nearest pharmacy to be filled. It takes a few days to arrive. Again, the protocols were in place to enable us to carry out the work safely and efficiently. We were allowed to prescribe several medications like some antibiotics, analgesia and creams and ointments. We learnt about the side effects of the medications and about allergies. There were instances when we can administer the controlled drugs at least once. Then we had to consult the doctor on call. We could start an intravenous infusion and again consult the doctor with all the relevant information.

We had to do a test once every three years on immunisations to keep abreast of any changes in the vaccination regime. With well baby checks, we also administered their immunisations. Mothers were provided with all relevant information regarding the immunisation, the side effects that a child may have and how best to minimise their symptoms of discomfort.

Many were the times when we had to look after people's pets too. Sometimes due to an accident, a dog usually had a broken limb, fishhook in its gob or, as I mentioned earlier, porcupine quills. Sometimes we do call a vet in the city to consult. Or once I did call our good friend a veterinarian in the UK for advice on a problem that a dog was having. She advised me to bring the dog in next morning. I had woken her up in the middle of the night! In the early years we also had to give the rabies injection and boosters to the dogs. If a nurse wasn't comfortable doing that, then she was by no means forced to do so. I personally enjoyed doing it. Then wildlife officers were employed in each community to do the yearly rabies injections. They also monitor that dogs do not run in packs. Dogs running in packs have been known to attack children and even adults in communities and sadly would eat them.

A German Shepherd had a fishhook in its lip. It had been nosing around in a box and he ended up with a hook in its lower lip. It was a gentle dog but it wouldn't let us near its mouth. A few men tried holding it down and, still being gentle, it struggled and whilst struggling, kept shaking its head, the hook fell off on its own. The dog was none the worse for its ordeal, but the men were sweating from tussling with the dog.

SAMY WILSON

Chapter 9
Medical Evacuation

Life-threatening emergencies are stabilised on arrival at the clinic and after assessment, the doctor on-call is consulted. The doctor will advise on treatment and a medevac is arranged. Depending on weather and medevac flight availability and, depending on where the community is, the flight can be as quick as an hour or hours. A plane might already be in the air and at times it can get diverted, rarely, to pick up a patient. But it has happened a few times. The medevac nurse may have a patient on board already and have space to pick up another patient. Or the flight is in the air after taking a patient home in some unusual circumstances; like a palliative care patient taken home to be with his family and familiar surroundings. It may even warrant a nurse from the community to go with the patient as well. This too has happened but not often. Permission is obtained from the nursing supervisor before a nurse goes off from the community. This means the community is a nurse short.

Emergencies could be any number of medical crises. It could be pre-term labour – most of the time the symptoms stop and the woman goes on to have a full-term delivery. Heart attacks are seen more often nowadays and with prompt treatment, the patient has a very productive, extended life in the north. The change in diet and lifestyle in the north in recent times could all be a contributory factor to heart disease. Babies, I found, were quick to worsen in a very short time. Accidents in the community or out on the land involving the all-terrain vehicles or a snowmobile or even the trucks, all could present us with a casualty. I remember going out on the land with a community lady in a SUV and a front wheel came off. We could have been in a nasty accident, but thankfully we were all right.

Three of us nurses and the community doctor responded to a tragic plane crash in a community I was in. The pilot and two passengers were killed and there was one survivor with a shoulder injury. We could do something for the survivor, but he was in terrible shock and I don't think his injury really bothered him as much as being a witness to the tragedy of his flying companions. Thankfully, our community doctor was there at the time and it took a weight off us. I will never forget their faces.

In recent years there has been a spate of glue and gas sniffing by children, in different communities. They are of various ages, some as young as seven and up to teenager years. There had been incidents of dropping a lit match into the fuel can and having their face close to the opening to see what's happening inside the can. A flashback happens. The fire causes burns to the kid's face and a lot of injury to the face and airways – singed eyelashes and scalp hair and facial burns and nose and lips burns (besides burning the hands holding the can). They drop the can causing a fire and the results of smoke inhalation, being trapped in a cabin. The kids are usually in a cabin out on the land by themselves or in a shed without adult supervision.

Such an incident happened in one community. We were already dealing with an emergency, but we were aware that there were a few people outside the clinic entrance but away from the entrance light. We assumed that they were relatives of the patient we were dealing with inside. Families turn up when a person is seriously ill and waiting to be medevacked. We had a medevac arranged and waited for the plane to arrive. I can't exactly remember how or who found out that there were some youths outside the clinic needing to be seen urgently. There were three girls, teenagers and they came in with burns to their face and hands and suffering from inhalation of smoke. All three were with different degree burns. One was worse but they were all talking and were walking around. We knew that one girl was going to need more care. They were seen to and the girl who was worse was not listening to advice to stay in bed either. That girl was eventually sedated and intubated by the doctor who was on the medevac and the medevac nurse was able to take the first patient as well. That first patient had acute renal failure, a middle-aged female and she needed hospital care as soon as possible. Sometimes that's how it goes. Sometimes there is only one patient to medevac and at times three or four. That would mean at least two flights.

Drug overdose was a frequent emergency that we dealt with in the communities; attempted suicides, a cry for help. A lot has been undertaken by the healthcare to try and meet the challenges of this mental health crisis. In an emergency the patient is medevacked out and whilst in the city, the mental health team would be very actively involved. Once in the community, it's a challenge to get the patient to attend counselling by the mental health nurse, if there is one in the community.

Gunshot wounds and stabbings or arms through a glass window too.

I haven't even mentioned the chronic diseases that becomes acute in many cases, like the chronic obstructive lung disease, heart diseases of different variety, diabetes and its complications creating emergency intervention and care at times.

Spontaneous abortion happens and most times the bleeding is well controlled but at times due to some remaining products in the uterus or the cervix of the womb, which is the neck of the womb, there is heavy bleeding. Intravenous fluids and medications to stop the bleeding is undertaken. Most times the patient is medevacked out to have surgery to clear the uterus.

Most of what we see in the north, I am sure are also seen in the accident and emergency departments of the southern cities. I haven't done much Accident and Emergency nursing in the south – only a few weeks during my nursing training in the early 70s. Working in the north all those years did give me quite a bit of experience. Working with some excellent experienced nurses helped in my learning.

Medical evacuations of patients are usually sent south to bigger city hospitals. From Labrador the patients are sent to St. Johns; from Manitoba and Nunavut to Winnipeg hospitals.

SAMY WILSON

Chapter 10
Urgent Nursing Cases

Some urgent cases may need attention straight away. Allergies and anaphylaxis need prompt intervention and treatment. Anaphylaxis is worrying and the patient is monitored in the clinic until they can go home with medications.

Dog-bites are taken seriously as rabies were sometimes detected in wildlife, like the foxes that comes into the community and bite a dog that's usually tied up; passing the rabies on to the dog. When someone comes in with a dog bite the history is taken to find out about the animal and if it was a dog that is usually tied outside. If so, then that dog is taken by the wildlife officer and if he suspects rabies then the dog is put to sleep and tested for rabies. In the meanwhile, the patient is started on prophylactic treatment that takes a number of days to carry out. The injections are available at all times in all the clinics of the north.

Patients with coughs over a period are screened closely for tuberculosis. Chest X-rays and sputum collection are carried out. Treatment is started only when the tests are confirmed. If tests reveal positivity, then the contacts are screened. Depending on the contacts' results and history, many may need to be started on TB meds. It is a great hive of activity when someone in the community has been tested positive for TB. Close living and overcrowding help in the spread of TB.

Diabetics when not controlled well, are managed and supported further with their treatments. Most of them are elderly and family members are given the teaching as well in regard to diet and medications. Some of the diabetics end up with kidney disease and are on peritoneal dialysis or haemodialysis. Patients who end up with peritoneal dialysis have extensive teaching at the city hospital with a relative who will be there for them all the time. They come home with all their needs to continue with their peritoneal dialysis at home and have a life at home in the community. Patients on haemodialysis are kept in the cities in accommodation with an escort. This is hard on the patient as well as on the escort. The escorts get to take a break and return home to see their family and another goes in to be an escort. Whether in future things will be different, is another scope of practice to mull over.

Seizure disorder, uncontrolled, is another problem we see and manage. Trying to get the patient to comply with taking the medication is a challenge at times.

Alcohol withdrawal is not urgent, but the patient is in great distress and agitated and making them comfortable with a few interventions does not take much from us. Simple treatment of intravenous fluids and vitamin B12 and having them at rest in clinic for a while helps. Sadly, some nurses do not see it the same way. I have noticed them withholding treatment that would ease their distress. We are not judge and jury to withhold that treatment. I tried to question this with the nurse. She gave me an explanation that I was not happy with either. I was not satisfied, but then I felt I shouldn't judge her either. Maybe "cruel" is a harsh word to describe the nurse. I can't even remember the explanation now. Everything worked out well in that case. From that time on I didn't much care for that nurse. Thank goodness it was only that one nurse who did that.

I loved suturing wounds. There were much suturing to be done in any given week. People sustain cuts and come in. Children are especially prone to getting cuts and bruises as all children do. Children play without looking out for the hazards that are everywhere. Sometimes using special glue or steri-strips might solve the problem if it is a small wound, but if the wound is big and bleeding then suturing of the wound is called for.

Asthma and chronic obstructive lung disease recurrences are also quite frightening for the patients and we usually deal with it most times quite effectively at the clinic. There had been many times when we had to ship a patient out as a medevac.

Nosebleeds most times are manageable and some take a while to manage (more on this later).

The patients who were a concern for the nurses are listed for the next visiting doctor. The doctor came once a month from Monday to Friday. The specialists like the Paediatrician, Psychiatrist, Obstetrician,

Internist and Ophthalmologist did their visits about two-three times a year in each community. The relevant patients were seen by them as well. Sometimes the visiting community doctor would refer patients out earlier to the different specialists in the cities, if warranted.

Chapter 11

Mental Health

This subject is not taboo anymore like it used to be at one time, thankfully. It affects most families in one form or another. The illness exists in all societies. Mental health like all illnesses, doesn't choose the person. Depression and schizophrenia in its various forms affect a lot of people. Addictions to alcohol and drugs make things worse for the patient. We all go through difficult periods in our lives at one stage or another. How a person copes and handles some of those periods have a lot to do with the kind of strength and support that a person has. Not all are able to cope effectively. Some families find it hard to cope with the illness in their loved ones. Who knows? They may be fighting their own demons.

Recently, I came to know one of the nicest and gentlest people I knew had committed suicide. It's heartbreaking. I know of many wonderful people who just can't seem to be helped and have committed suicide. What does it say of us as a society and the profession, that we haven't been able to solve that problem? There is always someone who has escaped our vigilance. It leaves us as professionals asking what we have missed. How could we have missed such a cry for help? Knowing that our loved one wished to leave us is hard to fathom for families. When there are children in the family, they find it harder to understand and throughout their lives they will wonder why their loved one left them in such a manner.

Even though there are regular visits by psychiatrist and mental health nurses, it doesn't appear to be enough. Schizophrenia treatment in the form of medication seem to be effective. I personally found the schizophrenia patients great to get along with. They seemed to have such a friendly manner, and most are able to articulate well. The problem is, they feel so well on medications, they feel they are cured and come off their medication by their own accord. When we follow them up to find out why they have not picked up their refill, they are adamant they are fine and do not need their medications anymore. Sometimes a patient may be convinced to continue the medication but some will simply say, "No more." This results in a waiting game to see them falling right back to their original state of manic. The whole process to get them back to be functioning people starts all over again. And it does take a while.

When there are no mental health or social worker in the community, it falls on the nurse during a mental health crisis to care for the patient. We consult with the on-call doctor at the end of a telephone with the crisis at hand. The doctor then consults the psychiatrist for further treatment. The system works. Depending which doctor returns to the community first, either the psychiatrist or the community doctor, the patient is seen. There are incidents of suicides in all communities. Men usually seem to hang themselves or use a gun on themselves. Attempted suicides are many. Whether by gunshot or drugs.

Even a ten-year-old was brought in with rope marks around his neck. He was trying to hang himself. What prompts such an act in one so young? Just by luck, an early intervention stopped him carrying out his intentions successfully.

Nurses have been attacked by patients, especially mental health patients. I knew a mental health nurse who was attacked. The patient used her fists to cause damage to the nurse's jaw. The nurse was off for a long time but did eventually return to work. She was confident and she had no fear that there would be a reoccurrence.

Another time there was a schizophrenia patient who assaulted a nurse. He had been off his medicines as well.

A young man just hated the people in authority, and he would go around slashing the vehicle tyres of the nurses and the RCMPs. In that community we lived away from the clinic and were dependent on the vehicle to get to the clinic in an emergency. We had to come out of the residence to get into the vehicle. There was no garage in that particular community for the clinic vehicle. Every time I got called out after hours, I would be wondering if I would be confronting the young man by the vehicle. When he came to the clinic, he would be the calmest and softly spoken young man and so easy to deal with. It was a contradiction that baffled people in authority.

A young woman who had a very sad upbringing would come to the clinic angry and would be swearing at me if she didn't get what she wanted. She would go away in a huff but would phone back, apologising, most politely. This happened a few times.

Overdosing on medication is something we see a lot of in the north and I wonder if it is the same in the south. Usually it's the young people, mostly female. Tylenol or anti-depressants are the most common drugs used. The new procedure does not involve stomach washouts like it did in the past. The northern clinics are well stocked with all the usual antidotes. Protocols are in place to treat and stabilise the patient before being medevacked south, where the mental health team will follow up the patient.

In one community there was a group of girls, six teenagers, who planned and took overdoses at the same time. That created major problems as there were only two nurses stationed there at that time. All hands-on deck was called for in that situation: the receptionists, the CHR, community health representative, the maintenance man and the relatives. The girls had planned that they would all be medevacked out simultaneously and they would be in the city together for a few days. They were all medevacked out and they returned all safe and well. Sometimes I do wish that the young people could have a break in the cities, or some sort of activity to keep them occupied. Most people have very few opportunities for getting employment as there are very few jobs in any northern community. Putting food on the table is costly for parents, let alone sending the kids out for a break.

One Boxing Day I was getting ready for bed when the phone rang and when I picked it up to say NOC, nurse on call, all the other voice said was, "You are there" and hung up. I didn't get an opportunity to ask or say anything else. Sometimes the NOC is out walking and leaves a message accordingly. I knew instinctively that it was an emergency. I quickly went and opened the door. I called my second on-call to come down as well. She was annoyingly difficult at that request and started quizzing me to what the emergency was, and I could only tell her exactly what I heard. She said that it could be someone coming in to hurt us for all she knew. That was sometimes a problem when you have a colleague you depend on who was being difficult. But she was also right about nurses sometimes being victims of assault. I had to resort to calling another nurse, who was a mental health nurse, to come down and stand by.

In a matter of minutes there came a few women carrying a young woman between them. At a later stage, I would wonder why there had been no man assisting them. The young woman was unconscious. The second on-call had been watching from her window and satisfying herself that it was an emergency, came down to help. She was a very experienced nurse who I had worked with a number of years previously and I had looked forward to working with her again. Administering all emergency care and at the same time questioning the mother who had also accompanied the woman, we found out she had swallowed the mother's antidepressants. She began to have a seizure. We were able to stabilise her until the medevac nurse and doctor arrived. She was medevacked out, sedated and intubated. By that time, it was morning. Without a doubt having "that difficult nurse" was a great help and very necessary. She came through when I needed help (more on her later when I talk about nurses). The young female patient stayed in the hospital in the south for a while seeing the mental health team. I was very happy to see her back in the community. She was a lovely-natured young woman with multiple problems.

There were numerous incidents that were similar and familiar, in most communities. Nurses who have stayed in a community for a long period get to know their community people well and know how to relate to the people very effectively. Over the number of years working in the various communities I got to know most people and worked well in the north.

Some adults with mental illness, I noted, had a very good command of the English language. I realised most of them could be the ones as children, who were parted from their families and dragged off to "residential schools" miles away, where they went through some life-changing hardships. They were abused so badly that they ended up mentally traumatised. They lost their language and were forced to learn another. They ended up learning and living a religion taught by unforgiving and unsympathetic men and women who did not follow their own teachings. So many died and were buried without their families knowing what happened to their young ones.

Recent shocking discovery of unmarked graves and burial sites were in the media. In May 2021, the remains of two hundred and fifteen children were discovered near Kamloops, BC. These were the First Nations people. The Inuit suffered similar fates. This prompted searches for more burial grounds. More sites are being discovered. Most returned home feeling very alienated in their birth communities and had to relearn their birth language – no doubt they learnt English and other things like cooking and cleaning. On their return to their communities, they had to learn to hunt and trap and provide for their families. Many are left with bitterness and sorrow for their lost years with their family. Many of their families would have died. These are not just Canada's northern tragedy but seems to be familiar happenings in different parts of the world as well.

A first cousin of mine in his late teens walked into the sea. He was the youngest and only boy with seven sisters. They loved him very much. He was a gentle soul. What demons must have prompted him to carry out such a deed!

An uncle, my mum's brother, shot himself over a love affair gone wrong. He was a police inspector. Another brother of my mum spent many years in a mental institute, and I cringe to think of the treatments he would have had in those days. My mother only had two brothers and they were handsome gentlemen. I have seen pictures of them. Mother would get upset talking about them. In fact, looking back at my own mum, I know she went through bouts of depression. She never saw a psychiatrist. That was how it was in those days. Any wonder! She had thirteen children. In later years she lived a peaceful life with her children and died on Christmas Day 2022 at the ripe old age of ninety-three.

When, as a nurse, you have been in a community long enough and gotten to know each person, there is a great trust placed in the nurse by the patient. They ground me, and "there, but for the grace of God, go I."

Chapter 12
Unexpected Cases

I want to share some more of my most memorable northern nursing experiences. They are not in chronological order. They are not in any order. In discussing the cases, the communities are not named. Patients are not identified. Nearly forty years in the north, I have been in various communities in Northern Manitoba, Labrador and Nunavut. Some northern nurses may not agree or have a similar view to mine, but I reiterate that these are my memories and my opinions. Again, to reiterate, it is not to be identified as any academic value or purpose. I would like to think that many will find it interesting. I found so many incidents very interesting and they stayed with me because of the people that I came to love and think highly of. Many nurses may identify similar cases that they may have come across and dealt with differently. These are my "reminiscences" and these are how I remember the cases.

I developed the skills as a northern nurse by learning from skilled and experienced nurses and doctors who are always willing to teach. The clinics and health centres have many manuals and books and old editions are always replaced with new editions to keep up with current changes. I don't claim to know many things. I don't claim to be an expert and stand corrected and humbled by the opportunities that came my way to learn; to be able to share with other nurses who may be contemplating working in the north and of the many soul-satisfying outcomes. I learnt from younger nurses who came with up-to-date information and present practices.

One very simple example that stood out to me is my friend, Leela. She said that when you are doing an ECG on a patient with chest pains, you always face the patient and never turn your back on the patient. A nurse will look at the machine, waiting for it to spew out the printing of the ECG. Nowadays they do spew out the prints, I mean. In my early years in the north, they were archaic and didn't. Since then, I never turn my back on a patient with chest pains when I am doing an ECG (in case the patient collapses without making a sound).

Over the years I came across some very interesting cases: some heartrending; some tragic and most with happy endings. It was always paramount to have professional concern for a worrying case and to make sure that everything is done methodically to ensure a positive outcome. I am a Hindu, but very much a believer that all of us have our own religious beliefs. In dire emergencies I say a silent prayer and mine is, "Whichever God is awake, please help me help the patient!" The other thing that kept me grounded was that any patient I saw, I thought that this patient could be one of my own family and in a similar situation, and I ensured they were well taken care of.

Many colleagues of mine have said to me that I am calm and collected in emergency situations. It didn't mean that my heart was not racing! In any emergency I was always ready to be in the forefront to help my colleagues as well. Probably some would have preferred that I kept out of the way!

My tales are not in any order either in the timeline or in the communities I have worked in. Some of the medical terms have changed over the years. I am sticking with what I knew then.

As a midwife I had seen pre-eclampsia in many prenatal patients and how they were cared for to avoid eclampsia. Signs and symptoms of pre-eclampsia is high blood pressure, protein in urine and oedema of lower limbs. In worsening cases, there were puffiness and abnormal weight gain, headaches and in imminent cases of eclampsia, seeing spots and a sensitivity to lights. Never for a moment did I think I would see a patient with eclampsia. Certainly not on that fine morning.

Any given morning we were always busy with patients wanting to be seen. That morning was no different. A middle-aged lady was telling the desk staff, the receptionist, that her niece was not well, and she needs to be seen at her home.

She was very softly spoken and was requesting gently that a nurse went to see her niece at home. The receptionist came to me, a new nurse in the community, and informed me of the request. Most of the people did not speak English. The young ones spoke English but found translating difficult. The aunt was quite sure that her niece was not able to come to the clinic. On questioning, with the receptionist translating, I found out that the niece was pregnant and when I checked her prenatal records, she had been well up to then and it was her first baby. Without further ado I informed the nurse in charge, who was also new to the community like me, that I should carry out a visit to the young lady in question. There were only the two of us nurses there. On setting out of the clinic with the receptionist, I found to my chagrin, the house was right next door to the clinic. In fact, it was shouting distance. I didn't say anything. I entered a brightly lit living room and found a few young women sitting around quietly. I was directed to the young woman in question, she did not appear to understand me at all, she looked jittery, and she did not answer any of my questions all the time I was looking at her and had the blood pressure cuff on her arm. The high reading shocked me, realisation hit me then that she was going to seizure any moment. I understood at the same time why she was really out of it. The receptionist who accompanied me was sent off to get the maintenance man and stretcher and warn the nurse in charge that we had an emergency. It took us less than five minutes and we had her on the clinic emergency bed, an intravenous line in and she started her seizures.

I had seen seizures before but nothing like that young woman's that day. We got the doctor on the line, and we managed to bring her blood pressure down quickly with medication and to treat her eclampsia. We were able to stabilise her. We kept vigil and kept her calm and the room darkened. She was medevacked out with a doctor and midwife who came on the medevac flight to escort her to the main hospital in the city. She was there till she was delivered of a healthy baby girl. When she returned to the community with her baby, I did not recognise her. She returned as a slim, beautiful young woman. The young woman who was medevacked out was a big bloated sick patient. Thankfully, it all ended well.

The same young woman soon became pregnant again and this time she had a close eye kept on her prenatally and it turned out a normal pregnancy and she had a normal delivery. On Boxing Day morning there was loud banging on the nurse's residence and when I opened the door, I was handed the three-month-old baby, unresponsive. We did try resuscitation but unsuccessfully, the baby was dead. Sudden Infant Death Syndrome, SIDS. It appears to happen sometimes sadly. She had a normal prenatal, with a normal delivery but ended up with a SIDS. Whereas she had eclampsia in her first pregnancy and that baby had no problems. It beggars belief.

There was a very sad case. I was examining a three-month-old baby at a well child clinic. As I usually do, I started undressing the baby and at the same time questioning the mother on how the baby was doing regarding his daily feedings and his bowel movements and micturition. I realised the baby was really looking skinny and lethargic. When I ran my hands on his scalp, I noted enlarged lymph nodes at the back of his head. Never have I felt enlarged lumps on a baby before. He had not gained weight. I was very concerned. I called the on-call doctor with my concerns and findings. A medevac was arranged. It was nearly twenty hours later before the medevac plane arrived. There were a few medevacs on the go that day. The baby survived a few days but died soon after whilst in hospital. He had cancer. I can't remember the exact type of cancer.

There are some cases that are unforgettable. Why these things happen to little babies is difficult to comprehend.

Chapter 13
A Rare Thing

Sometimes a family member requests that a nurse comes out to the land, where people are out camping, to see a sick relative. Usually in the spring when the weather gets warmer; the people put up their tents far out on the land and make it very cosy, with spruce branches on the ground that radiates with the smell of pines. They wait for the geese to fly in. I have been fortunate enough to visit people in their camps at times. You are made most welcome.

I was asked to go out on the land to see a sick woman, whom the family felt was too sick to be moved. A community member was ready to take me and, because it was not a working day, the maintenance man who would usually take the nurse on such expeditions was away somewhere out on the land as well. So I set out with this community member on his snowmobile and hauling a komatik behind (a sort of sled). I had all the necessary emergency equipment in the komatik. Within a short while of leaving the community, we met with our first hurdle. The snowmobile was being driven in water that was thawed on top of the lake. I did have my rubber boots on with thick socks. The man stopped and advised me to walk away from the snowmobile to the tree line, near the water's edge. I have no idea why he told me to do that. I did as advised. I had no fear because I had no clue that it was risky. "Where ignorance is bliss, 'tis folly to be wise" (Thomas Gray). I remember it as a beautiful sunny spring day and quite warm. After that, we kept to the edge of the lake and eventually got to the lady. She was quite ill. After assessing her, we brought her back to the community on the stretcher in the komatik we had taken with us. I remember the journey back was a slow one as the snowmobile driver was careful over bumps and he tried to avoid them. Once in the community and having done a thorough check again on the lady, I consulted the doctor on call with the findings. She was medevacked out. She died soon after, while in hospital from Miliary TB. It really was a unique case. I knew she was sick, but she didn't look like she was dying the day I medevacked her. Miliary TB is a rare condition. Not every doctor or nurse gets to see a case in their lifetime. I got to see another case (not that I knew what it was until he had been diagnosed in hospital) many years later in another community which I will talk about next:

I had arrived that day at the community and the nurse in charge asked if I would mind seeing a patient who had been frustrated with the nurses. I knew the community well and the patient in question too. He spoke English well. Many though need a translator present. The patient proceeded to tell me that he had been unwell: poor appetite, losing weight and general malaise. He had a slight cough. He was requesting to be sent out to see a doctor at the nearest hospital. The visiting doctor wasn't due for a while. Blood work and sputum had been sent out and we awaited results. The man genuinely felt ill, and I knew he was not a man who came to the clinic unnecessarily. I checked with the nurse in charge and consulted the doctor on call, who was advising me that I should wait for the results and wait for the community doctor to see him in the community. I had to submit the case that the patient felt he needed to be assessed by the doctor soon. In the end, the doctor agreed but the patient was to fly out on a regular flight instead of a medevac.

The desk staff were very good and they managed to get two seats for the patient and his escort on the schedule flight. He was sent out with a family escort. He was in the hospital for a few days. All the tests were repeated at the hospital and the few results that came in first didn't show anything of note. The doctor was thinking of discharging him. The patient got very upset and got out of bed and collapsed at the doctor's feet. I heard this from the escort at a later date. He went into a coma. Then the rest of the results were chased up and he was diagnosed with Miliary TB. The patient survived – a miracle. He was in a coma for nearly a year and eventually ended up in a wheelchair and lives in a care home in the city. He is not able to speak either but able to recognise his relatives when they visit him.

Sometimes it is frustrating for the nurses as well when we can't send out a patient as the patient wants, to seek further care from a doctor. When a doctor is in the community, the doctor would try to go through the list of patients that are listed. Sometimes not all the patients get seen. Delays happen due to bad weather, or emergencies that have happened while the doctor is in the community, taking the doctor away from seeing the list of patients who are scheduled. The doctors have other commitments to go on to, leaving patients unseen in the community. This causes a lot of aggravation and unhappiness all around. No number of explanations and reassurances are accepted by the patients. Understandably.

One morning even before the clinic was due to open, a young woman phoned to say she wanted to bring her mother in as she wasn't feeling well. Knowing that her mother was a diabetic and not at all well controlled, I agreed that she can bring her mother in. The patient was very non-compliant with her meds and diet. No amount of counselling seemed to help and she always had reasons for her non-compliance. I still liked her and her family though and had a lot of time for them.

She could hardly walk when she came in. She had a massive abscess on one of her buttocks extending down to her perineum. She had a fever and her blood sugars were out of whack. Consulting the doctor with all my findings, the doctor was going to let her stay in the community and to treat her with IV antibiotics. It took me a bit of convincing the doctor that she needed to be medevacked and be seen at a hospital. She was medevacked out. She was diagnosed with Necrotizing Fasciitis – a flesh eating disease. She had surgery to excise the infected tissue. Intravenous antibiotics of the New Generation. She was there for quite a while and by the time she came home, the wound was a smaller area to dress.

Surprisingly, I never came across a patient with HIV or AIDS. Neither as a midwife, nor as a northern nurse. Whenever we had a patient with a sexually transmitted disease we checked their blood for HIV, Syphilis, Hepatitis B as the protocol indicates and with the patients consent, which they readily agree to. Most of the time the patients only had Chlamydia. Gonorrhoea rarely. Genital warts at times.

The worst genital wart infection I had come across was in a very young pregnant woman, when I was a midwife in the late 70s in UK. She was in her teens and was admitted for the treatment of her warts. She went through agony with the treatment. Looking back, I wonder why she had to go through such painful treatment. I didn't see it clearing at all. Maybe that was the only treatment in those days. She went on to have a caesarean section to prevent her delivering vaginally.

I sincerely hope that such treatments are much more humane now.

SAMY WILSON

Chapter 14

What a Child Sees

The first night in a community and on call, I was called by a family member to say a young woman had shot herself. She was not able to bring her to the clinic. I called the driver allocated to help us drive to the house. He came to get me and got all the emergency equipment loaded and within minutes we were out the door and at the house which was not far. The house was dimly lit and quiet. I wondered if we were at the right house. I saw the young woman on the couch at the far end of the living room. Her eyes were wide open as I walked in. I thought she was dead.

When I got close to her, I realised she was alert and was watching me approach. She responded to my queries whilst I checked the bullet wound on her abdomen. There was hardly any bleeding, yet I noted the bullet hole. I quickly assessed her and got her on to the stretcher and brought her to the clinic. With the second nurse on call, we did a thorough check and found the exit wound at her back. There was still hardly any bleeding externally. We got an intravenous line in. All her vital signs were very stable, and I consulted the doctor on call. A medevac was arranged. She was started on IV antibiotics. This was around 10pm. The medevac plane came around five in the morning by which time her abdomen was tense, and she was having a high fever. She was very agitated. She had internal bleeding as suspected and expected. She was in hospital for a long while and returned with a colostomy which was reversed a year later.

The young woman whilst intoxicated, had shot herself in front of her young seven-year-old son. When she was pregnant with her son; her boyfriend, the father of her son, whilst intoxicated, had shot himself fatally in front of her. It was sad that her young son had to witness the shooting. The child was followed up closely with mental health counsellors.

A middle-aged woman once told me of her tragic childhood memory. On a winter's day she had been at a relative for a sleepover as her parents were drinking at home. She got up in the morning and as the house was next door, she went home. Just inside the front door, on the ground, she found her mother dead. She remembered her mother being covered in blood, having been beaten up by her dad. She was seven years old. She had gone back to get the relatives who were still asleep. How does a child ever forget such a scene? What a way to remember her mother! I had great affection for this lady even before I knew about this tragic incident. She had a lovely, mild manner. She indeed had a hard life with her husband who was just as abusive as her father had been to her mother. Her eldest daughter was also abused by the husband, the father of her daughter. Some people sadly cannot seem to escape such sad sufferings. Only death seems to release their pain.

I have seen a few shotgun wounds whilst working in the north. Many are attempted suicides. One night, I was awoken with loud banging on the door. The person behind the door was sobbing loudly. I was terrified – more with the sobbing than anything. Within seconds so many thoughts were flashing through my mind. Is that the nurse on call sobbing at the door? Who has hurt her? Is the person with her? I did not hesitate though and opened the door. It was a sister of a young chap who had shot himself and the nurse on call needed help and had sent her to get me. Sending a silent prayer of gratitude that the nurse wasn't harmed, I went to assist. The young man had inflicted a wound to his abdomen. He was stable and it did look like a superficial wound. He was medevacked out. It was his second attempt. He returned home after counselling and to continue counselling in the community by a mental health nurse. My memory of that banging on the door and the fright I had, will stay with me forever, I think.

A very sad memory of a middle-aged man shooting himself still troubles me to this day. It's hard to fathom how a loved one can come to such a decision leaving behind tortured questions that no one can honestly answer. It leaves me to this day questioning myself: What else could have been done?

When I was a student nurse in the early seventies, we had to choose to do a three-month stint at either obstetrics, psychiatric, paediatrics or geriatrics. I was young and didn't like psychiatry, but I thought I will try it anyway. Whilst I was doing it, I became quite depressed. The one person who stood out for me to this day is a young woman who was severely depressed. She had been sexually abused by her father since childhood and now she was a resident at the psychiatric hospital. This was in the days when patients can be safe in the environment where they are treated and supported and where they can be monitored and ensure they eat and keep clean (this is my opinion, of course).

The patients are allowed out during the day for day trips. As a new foreign student nurse, during my days off, I was looking at the surrounding countryside of the UK. I wanted to visit Canterbury. I was a student nurse in Dartford, Kent, Joyce Green Hospital. The young woman was happy to travel to Canterbury with me to see the sights. We went by train. At one point she said she wanted to jump out of the moving train. I was shocked and just looked at her. I was an inexperienced nurse with no clue what to do next. I can't remember saying anything but just looked at her. And I wonder if my mouth was open as well. She didn't jump. I think she took pity on me and stopped her shenanigans for that moment. I remember very little of that trip to Canterbury. Towards the end of my nursing training, I found out she had successfully carried out her suicide. She had attempted suicide numerous times in her past. Her face has always stayed with me all these years. She was a beautiful young woman with so much sadness in her. Sadly, she couldn't cope with life anymore.

On a fine spring day when the snow is still on the ground and kids were tobogganing, a young five-year-old girl sustained a laceration to her thigh. A part of a tree, sticking up in the snow tore her thigh. She must have come off her toboggan. Her father carried her in. She was frightened and was crying and wouldn't let us remove her padded pants which were torn, and there was blood, but not bleeding much. After a lot of coaxing and reassurance by the clinic support staff, we managed to get her pants off. She kept her panty on. I was able to clean and suture her. She was at least allowing me to do that. It needed quite a few sutures. Whilst I was doing that, I noted her panty was very dirty and smelly. All the time I was suturing her I realised that the laceration to her thigh was not as big a problem as what I began to suspect. After sorting her laceration, I asked her dad if he has noticed any problems that his daughter was having to have such a dirty panty. He agreed that he has noticed she was having a lot of discharge "from below." He bathes her daily he said and she was notably very clean otherwise. With his permission the support staff was able to get her panty off and by this time she was quieter and co-operative. I was shocked at the copious amount of discharge. I was able to obtain swabs and urine samples to be sent off. The long and short of it was, the little girl had venereal disease and the father was abusing his little girl. The mother had left the marriage and left the little girl behind with her father. He was charged with abusing his little girl, the last I heard.

These are difficult cases to deal with and it shouldn't happen to little children. It happens though sadly, more frequently than we realise. There have been quite a few similar cases I had to deal with over the years.

Chapter 15

Miracles and Tragedy

During a routine clinic day, we might have unexpected emergencies that we have to attend to immediately and so interrupt our normal clinic day; especially, if a mother comes in first thing in a morning with her baby.

I remember the day was a Lab Day. That means we had patients booked in for bloodwork in the morning. It had to be done in the morning so that all the lab work will be ready to be sent out on the plane. We were busy when I noticed the mother with her baby in the waiting room. I felt an overwhelming anxiety seeing the mother with her baby and a premonition that something was not right.

I stopped what I was doing and called the mother in with the baby. She proceeded to tell me the problem whilst I was undressing the baby. I realised the baby's eyes were moving around jerkily. The baby was starting with seizure activity and was on the verge of collapse. I called my colleague in telling her we had an emergency. She managed to get the intravenous canula in at which point, the baby collapsed. We worked on the baby then. We got the on-call doctor on the line for consult. We were also waiting for the doctor who was scheduled to arrive on the plane that morning, around ten. It was before nine and one of the staff took off to the airport to get the doctor when she came off the plane. They did not wait for her luggage. The doctor came and we were working on the baby till the medevac plane, Lifeline, came in around five in the evening with a doctor, a respiratory therapist and a nurse. They did not leave until seven, two hours later with the baby. It was a very hard long day. The doctor was a very competent young lady who I had the pleasure of working with in the past. We did not see another patient all that day because we couldn't leave the emergency room. We did use the bathroom facility. The baby was out for months. In hospital she had all the complications that was going: meningitis, septicaemia to name just two. She was medevacked out a very sick baby. She came home well recovered.

I had worked with this doctor previously and the night before the baby event, I was going over in my mind about the last time we had worked together over a very sad event. I was hoping that this visit would be uneventful. On that occasion a young lad had been brought in on a winter's evening. He had been accidentally run over by a car. We had worked hard to revive him with no success. It was a very sad day.

I asked the doctor if she remembered her last visit. She admitted to remembering that sad day and was hoping for uneventful clinic days on this visit. There were three of us nurses and the doctor working on the young boy. I remember coming out of the emergency room at one point and looking at the waiting room. The waiting room was solid with people but there was not a single sound. When we had finished in the emergency room and with the police, we were quite drained. The maintenance man and his wife turned up and told us to leave everything and they would clean and tidy the emergency room. It was after midnight. We just put on our thick parkas and stepped out into the night to look at the sky. It was brilliant. The northern lights were dancing in the sky. The sky was studded with stars and there were even shooting stars. It was as if the heavens were welcoming the young lad. That's what my heart and mind was saying to me. When we came in from the cold we went into the garage where the maintenance man and his wife were waiting to say goodnight. They told us that they had just seen a white dove in the garage and when they opened the garage door it flew away. They were quite sure of what they had seen. I always wondered what they had seen. They knew a white owl from a dove. They are Inuit. They knew their wildlife.

A parent (or parents) bringing in a baby with seizures is a regular occurrence. Most of the time it's because of high fevers. Sometimes there are no reasons for the seizure. The baby is followed up by either the community doctor or the paediatrician depending on who arrives first in the community. Most of the time, a baby will not have any more seizures, but some continue with seizures throughout their lives and are on medication.

A beautiful female teenager was carried in by her dad, dead. She was an epileptic on medications. That morning they had gone into her bedroom to see why she was not up for school and found her unresponsive. She must have had a seizure during the night and choked to death. There was no postmortem required and she was buried in her hometown.

The north's permafrost makes digging the ground difficult and the dead are buried in shallow graves and rocks piled on top to prevent animals disturbing the graves.

Chapter 16
Country Food

People of the Canadian North love their country food (food they get from their land and sea). Eating raw meat is also part of their culture. Some of the wildlife are infected with Brucellosis and Trichinosis; botulism toxins, in rare cases from raw fermented meat. Personally, I never came across patients with Botulism but knew when a few people became infected in one northern community.

Brucellosis is seen about two to three times a year in one of the communities I used to work in for a number of years. It was usually found in the caribou herd population. A swollen scrotum and joints would alert the hunter that the caribou is infected. The hunter having killed the animal, would usually try to burn the carcass to prevent wildlife from eating it. Like foxes and ravens and dogs. Sometimes when there are no signs of the disease the meat is brought home and consumed. Raw meat is loved and preferred by the Inuit and if the meat is infected, then the person gets ill. Cooking the meat well, destroys the bacteria.

Usually when a person has been infected with Brucellosis, the person comes in with vague symptoms of aches and pains and fatigue. The symptoms do not appear right away but a good few days later. If it's a man, he usually has pains in his scrotum as well. Blood results take a while to be screened. Thankfully, the disease is treatable. But I have known, especially men, have the symptoms for a prolonged length of time – over a year even after treatment, which is also a lengthy one. They are closely followed up by the community doctor.

A very hardworking man came in complaining of chest pains. Having had previous open heart surgery a couple of years earlier, he was concerned. He was back to full-time employment and was in his sixties. His complaints were very specific. The pains were in the upper part of his sternum only. There were no radiating pains and no shortness of breath. There was no worsening of the pains with exertion, either. The pain was tolerable but constant. He had no fever and no redness at site of pain, even with firm palpation he only had discomfort.

We carried out all the relevant assessments including an ECG and couldn't identify anything untoward. We initially tried treatment with analgesia advising him to return if any worsening or if he had no relief. He returned with pains but no worse after a few days, and I went through the whole assessment process in case I have missed something. We repeated the ECG which was satisfactory. An X-ray and blood work were done. The patient was listed for the community doctor on his next visit to the community and was seen in due course with all the blood and X-ray results and another new ECG. The doctor couldn't find anything wrong either other than he had sternal pains and again was advised to continue with the analgesia but to return if he still had the pains. He did return and by this time I was concerned, as he was not a person to complain like he was doing. He was a very hard worker.

I decided to consult with the cardiologist who did his heart surgery. The normal practice was to go through the community doctor on call. I was connected to the cardiologist easily enough and at first, he was amiable and then he wasn't, and he wanted to know, rightly so, why I wasn't consulting with my own community doctor. I brought him up to date with all that's gone on hence far and how the man continues to experience the sternal pains. He was no worse, but neither was he better. He agreed to see him in his clinic in the city and arrangements were made to send him out on a regular flight. He went relieved to be seen by his cardiologist and so was I. I got a call a few days later from the Northern Patient Co-ordinator in the city, who co-ordinates all the northern patients who go down to the city for medical services. She proceeded to tell me about a phone call she had with the cardiologist who had asked her to share his call with me. He had also mentioned to the co-ordinator that he was initially dissatisfied with my consulting him. Since then, he had seen the patient and admitted him for further investigations. During the process he had consulted a visiting specialist from the Southern Americas. The man was finally diagnosed with localised infection of Brucellosis in his sternum. I am sure it was a first with the cardiologist too. He was kept in the city for intravenous antibiotics of the new Third Generation kind. I was pleased to have received the phone call and relieved that at long last the patient had a proper diagnosis and was being treated. I was glad as well that I took my patient's complaint seriously and went that little bit overboard for him. Knowing the people in the community helps. The men folk hunt caribou for the meat and he could have contracted the disease by coming into contact with Brucellosis contaminated caribou meat. In Labrador I came across "seal finger." This was an infection sustained from a cut from an infected seal, while cutting it up and harvesting the seal pelt. The hand can get very swollen and painful and the infection can radiate up to the arm. Long term treatment with Tetracycline works well. People use the seal pelt for sewing garments for their use.

Trichinosis is another infection that I have come across in the north. Trichinosis parasite is usually found in bear and walrus meat in Nunavut. As the Inuit like to consume raw meat and when there are clusters of people experiencing similar symptoms; a history of consumption of either bear or walrus meat, are ascertained and bloodwork screening starts. When the results are positive, the wildlife officer follows up with identifying the offending carcass and if available usually the tongue is isolated and sent off for analysis. Cooking the meats well, kills the parasites. Treatment of the disease works well.

Drying fish on clothesline looks like an art. The act of "drying" preserves them and they can be carried around easily when the people go out on the land. Foraging for berries in season is another country food the northerners depend on. So do the geese

and the wild animals. The vast land seems to provide
for all.

SAMY WILSON

Chapter 17

Mishaps on the Ice

A lesson I learnt was, what looks deceptively like a lot of blood, really is a small amount. Though I found out as well a patient could very well be bleeding internally and very little seen externally. To this day I still find active bleeding a little daunting.

A man came in one fine winter's day. He had been ice fishing, and he said he had hurt his hand. He had been drilling to make a hole in the ice and the drill had accidentally pulled out of his hand causing an injury. He was well dressed in his winter gear, including the homemade gloves which were especially warm. As I was helping him remove his gloves, with one of the gloves, a string slid out. The string was still attached. A finger was missing from his hand. I tipped the glove out and the finger popped out. The finger was quickly washed and wrapped in sterile wet gauze and placed in the fridge. His hand was cleaned and well wrapped up as well. Thankfully, that day a doctor was in the community clinic and he was soon in contact with a surgeon in the city and the patient got transferred to the city with his finger in a cooler box. The finger was stitched back, and he healed well.

Many accidents happen on the ice. I remember a young man whose snowmobile broke down and he was in wet snow and froze his toes and had to have some of his toes amputated. He had dressings done for a lengthy time till he healed.

A good friend of mine and I were walking one winter's day when she slipped on the ice and fell. She was in an awful lot of pain and had to have a strong analgesia for her pain. She got herself crutches and was limping around and went back to work limping around. Eventually she got an X-ray and found she had a spiral fracture in one of her lower legs. She went out to see a doctor in the hospital and returned with a cast and continued working, hobbling around. She was always quite stoic.

An elderly man whilst out alone on a winter's day checking his traps, turned his snowmobile on uneven terrain and got thrown off his machine. How he managed to straighten his machine and get himself home just tells you what the northerners are made of. He walked up the stairs and sat down and didn't want to move after that. I was called to the house and found him calm, and he was able to recount his ordeal quite clearly and appeared not to have had any other injury. Assessing him, it seemed like he had cracked a couple of his ribs and that's painful. I consulted with the community doctor and since that community didn't have an X-ray facility, he was sent out for an X-ray and assessment by the doctor. He did have a couple of fractured ribs on X-ray but otherwise no other injury. He came home with analgesia and recovered well in time.

Two young women were out walking one winter's day. A snowmobile with a komatik carrying a full load of logs swung out on the icy path and hit one of the women who fell and couldn't get up because of the excruciating pain she was having in one of her legs. She wasn't far from the clinic, and we, the nurses and maintenance man, fetched her on a stretcher and got her on the emergency bed. We had to cut her boots off, as hauling the boots off wasn't an option. She was in that much pain and we were unsure of what damage she had sustained from the hit. Even without an X-ray we realised she had a good compound fracture. The community doctor was in town, and she helped us to get a plaster cast on whilst we were waiting for the medevac plane. She was alright otherwise. The poor man who was driving the snowmobile was most upset that he had caused such an accident and was at the clinic until the medevac plane came for the young woman. It was an unexpected accident.

A couple of men went out one winter to hunt for seals on a snowmobile. The snowmobile broke down and they couldn't get it going. They also only had one gun between them. Usually, the practice was to stay with their broken-down machine. But the younger guy took off with the gun to walk back and wouldn't listen to the older guy to stay put. In the community a search party was initiated when after a reasonable amount of time the two party members didn't return. They eventually found the older guy crawling on the ice towards them. The search party thought it was a seal on the ice. He was brought to the clinic, and he was in a reasonable state but all he was concerned about was the younger man's whereabouts. He was medevacked.

The younger man was eventually found on an ice floe, and he was winched to safety by a search and rescue helicopter. He was next to a dead polar bear. The bear had tapped him to see if he was alive and the young fellow had woken up and shot it dead. There was a cub with it, and it stayed with the dead mother. It was better not known what may have happened to the cub I suppose. I never asked. The young man had frozen some of his toes and had them amputated. He came home and had dressings done daily for a long time and he healed well. The older man came home after a few days in hospital but had to be medevacked out within a few days of return with acute abdominal pains. He had abdominal surgery and found to have sections of his intestines had been frozen and was necrotic. He tolerated the surgery well and came home with a colostomy. The surgery was reversed after a year.

So many incidents like the above happen more frequently than we know. Having a snowmobile breaking down in a storm and way out on the land or sea ice is quite common but if there are more snowmobiles travelling together, then it would be relatively safer. That's usually the way people travel in the north or someone knows who is travelling where and what time they should have shown up. All very well organised.

Chapter 18

Creating Angels on Blood

Intoxication brings out in some people to throw out their inhibitions and to behave wildly and erratically. Whereas they may in everyday life work and live normally, there are many with underlying sadness and tragic lives of childhood, hitting the bottle at times to forget, giving them a chance to overlook their past traumas. They can voice their frustrations and sadness in their alcoholic state. I have encountered adults, besides the youth, still cutting themselves – usually females – and young men putting their arms through glass windows and/or assaulting one another and creating havoc and causing injury.

I was called to a house one morning for a woman who had been injured and she was bleeding. For whatever reason, she was refusing to come to the clinic. Arriving at the house, I found both husband and wife had been drinking all night and been fighting with each other and the husband had beaten her up. The wife was lying on the floor, awake and moving her arms around on the bloody slippery floor like she was making angels on snow. It was funny but really nothing to laugh about. She was very co-operative and allowed me to help her sit up and clean her up a bit to check where the bleeding was. There was a small wound on her scalp but with all the blood on the floor one would have thought she had a massive wound. I sutured her wound. All the while the husband was quiet and so was the wife, who was very compliant and meek and hardly spoke. I liked the couple. When sober, they are most charming and sociable people. Though that day, they were quiet as mice whilst I was there. As requested, she returned to the clinic for follow up next day, sober. I still remember them with great affection.

Monday mornings are usually busy. I happened to pass the patient's toilet and the door was open. A young man was at the sink, I suspected he was feeling nauseous. I stood at the doorway to ask if he was alright. The next instant he just spewed out blood quite explosively on to the sink and the wall above the sink. It looked horrendous. The nurse in charge was right next door, we got him onto the emergency bed. We had an emergency – intravenous fluid, oxygen and getting vital signs and at the same time trying to get a history from the young man who had come in alone. He had been vomiting blood at home and continued to bring up small amounts of bloody vomitus. Over the weekend he had been binge drinking alcohol and he looked like he had Esophagitis that could be fatal. He was medevacked out and after a few days he was back home with medication. One of my younger brothers was not so lucky. At age forty-three he did the same and bled out within minutes. He was admitted to the hospital at the time with abdominal pain. He died at a very young age.

A young twelve-year-old, driving an ATV (All-Terrain Vehicle) bumped over a rock and flew off it and nearly scalped himself. He walked into the clinic by himself and was able to clearly state what happened. He had bleeding from a scalp wound but minimal. On examination, I noted the skin of his scalp was partially peeled from the back. All his vital signs were stable. I cleaned the area well to assess, so I could notify the doctor on call of my findings and hoping she would approve a medevac. I couldn't determine if he had a skull fracture. If he was in the city, he would have an X-ray of his skull as a matter of urgency at least. The doctor recommended that the scalp be irrigated well. She advised me to suture the flap back in place and observe him for a couple of hours at the clinic and, if no further complications, he could be sent home.

As advised, I did irrigate the area well, inserted only about three sutures, just to keep the edges together. The doctor did not feel the need for an evacuation at that point as he did not have the signs of "basilar skull fracture." There were no bruising behind the ears. I wasn't satisfied. I kept him in for the night, monitoring him regularly. After two hours I noted the signs of bruising. His vital signs were stable. When I informed the doctor, she suggested I send him home and follow him up in the morning. I didn't feel comfortable at all and kept him in until the morning. He was stable. In the morning I called the doctor on call who would be a new one on duty. There was always a possibility that the new doctor on call would back what the previous doctor did. The young patient's report was given. She approved the medevac straight away and he was in the city for assessment and skull X-rays. He was monitored for a good few days in hospital for observation and came home none the worse. The doctor did discuss the event with the night doctor as well on the same day. So many things go through my mind about what could happen if he did have a scalp fracture and/or bleeding in his brain. Thankfully, the twelve-year-old was fine.

Nosebleeds are my worst nightmare and worried me a lot. Some are regular bleeders. It takes a long time to get some nosebleeds under control. Children with nosebleeds didn't worry me as much as the older ones.

A woman came in one day with a heavy nosebleed. As luck would have it, there was a doctor in the community. With great expertise the doctor was able to pack her one nostril and left the packing in overnight and she was kept in overnight because she did have a heavy nosebleed. Next day she looked stable, and all her vital signs were normal. The doctor decided to remove the packing and when she did, the blood gushed from her nostril. After that, no amount of packing, catheter procedure or cauterisation, stopped her bleeding. Her intravenous fluids were going in fast. The doctor decided to medevac her. Both the doctor and I escorted the patient on the plane to the city. The plane was like a war zone with bloodied gauze everywhere. We got her to the hospital and her bleeding was cauterised in the operating theatre. A few days later, she returned home as right as rain.

One middle of a night case; a young woman had called to say she can't stop her bleeding. I had woken up from a deep sleep and I am not sure if I asked her all the relevant questions. I thought she had cut herself with an ulu, a kind of a knife the Inuit people use to cut most things. It is not unusual for the Inuit to have a late-night snack of thinly sliced frozen, raw meat. The patient was quite insistent that her bleeding needed to be attended to. As I reiterated previously – knowing people of the community helps. I knew her and I realised that she wouldn't call unless she was worried about her bleeding. So, I advised her to come over. I got down to the clinic and assembled all the necessary items for suturing, which I was most comfortable with.

None of the houses are very far from the clinic even though not everyone had transport. I waited and waited and an hour later she turned up. She walked in by herself and I did not see any dressing anywhere on her hands. When I proceeded to ask why she was so late, she said she tried having a bath to see if the bleeding would stop but it didn't. On further questioning where she was bleeding, she said, "down there" indicating with her head toward her nether regions. She wasn't pregnant even though she was a young single woman. I got her to lie down on the examination bed and noted the bright red bleeding on her pad and proceeded to do a vaginal speculum exam. As I was inserting the speculum, I couldn't believe what I was seeing. The only way I could describe it was like a mini shower of blood from her upper part of her vagina. I realised that I had an emergency, and I called my second on-call colleague to come and help me.

An intravenous line started, and we tried to pack her vagina. Her vital signs remained stable and consulting with the doctor on call, a medevac was arranged. She went out and was seen, came back a couple of days later none the worse for her ordeal. We never found out the reason for her bleed. Some questions are never answered.

Many's the time, women have been carried into the clinic passed out at home having spontaneous abortions. As an emergency, oxygen would be started and an intravenous line started and fluids pushed. Treatment commenced to stop the bleeding by trying to contract the uterus. Sometimes it takes a while and we have to get the patient stable. Sometimes there are products of conception stuck in the cervix that is visible and if possible extracted. The on-call doctor is consulted and the patient was usually medevacked out. Most of the time they don't need any intervention but sometimes they have a surgery to clear the uterus.

A patient had internal haemorrhoidal surgery, rubber band ligation of the haemorrhoids, in the city. She had been discharged and had come home. She went out on the land with her family and started to bleed rectally. When they brought her in, she was bleeding bright red, just flowing out. The rubber band had come undone, and she was bleeding profusely. Again, intravenous fluids and attempting to stamp the flow of blood with packing, was near impossible.

Medical evacuation was arranged, and she was back in the city. She had many units of blood and IV fluids. By the time she left the clinic she was bloated with the fluids. The clinics do not stock blood, but the medevac nurses would bring the blood with them and start the blood infusion before leaving the clinic. The patient returned after further treatment of her haemorrhoids, looking like her old self.

When patients return home well recovered, there is a great satisfaction that as a profession we had provided our best service.

SAMY WILSON

Chapter 19

The Lady Knew She Had Cancer

Some are very sad outcomes. In one satellite community, there was a lady who was simply a lovely-natured soul – always with a welcoming smile on her face and always with kind words to say. One evening the lady called the nurse on call, requesting a Ventolin puffer because she was finding it hard to breathe. The nurse on call checked her chart and couldn't find anything regarding a respiratory problem in the past and she's never had a puffer before. Due to the distance and lateness of the hour, she was not able to get to the clinic. I was away to the nearest town for a course and because the nurse was new to the place, called me to check on what was the best way to go about the lady's problem. I decided to call the patient myself. The lady could speak clearly and proceeded to tell me she has breast cancer and was finding it difficult to breathe. I was flabbergasted. She had been calm and very matter of fact about it. We talked and she was happy to come to the clinic next morning to see me as I would be home on the early flight back. She got a Ventolin puffer for the night from the lay dispenser in her community with advice on its use.

People of this community are solid, down to earth, hardy souls. They can bear with great fortitude a lot of hardships and pains without complaining. I wanted to get back to see her first and check her and reassure her that she was wrong and she didn't have cancer. She was on my mind that night and I had a terrible premonition that I couldn't shake off.

Thankfully, the plane flew on time and when I got to the clinic straight from the flight, the lady was there with her beautiful, calm, serene smile. I was so happy to see that she was looking so well and none the worse for her breathlessness.

My happiness was short lived. When I got to examine her and found that she did have all the obvious signs of advanced stage breast cancer. She had "peau d'orange" (like the skin of an orange) of one breast and lumps under her armpit. Sadness overwhelmed me and I could have cried. But I do get this bland look on my face when I don't want to show what I am thinking. The lady had been looking at me intently the whole time I was assessing her, which wasn't long. She took everything in her stride. After consulting with the doctor, who arranged to see her in town where he was based, travel arrangements were made for her and her daughter as an escort, to go out. From there she went on to see the oncologist in the city. She went through her treatments like the trouper she was. She did well for a few years and then she died in her own community with her family around her. I will never forget the lady nor her family.

How resilient people are in that community reminds me of another case. Many years later, the sister of the breast cancer lady had a fall on her boat whilst fishing with her husband. She was getting a pail of water, she had slipped and fell on the upper edge of the boat, hitting herself on the left upper abdomen. It was a summer's day. She called me a day after the incident, hoping the pain will resolve on its own. She was stoic but the unbearable pain only worsened and she was plagued with dizzy spells as well. Even though she was calm on the phone I realised she was in a bad way when she said she couldn't travel down on the boat to see me in clinic. I always think of the very worst scenario and then find it a great relief that it's not, after all, a major life-threatening issue.

In my mind I sort of worked out that she has caused grievous harm to her spleen. The maintenance man and I set out on the boat for the satellite community. The clinic had a boat that was well-maintained all the time in case of emergencies like this and for our regular weekly clinic visits during the summer months. The maintenance men are usually from the community where they are born and bred. They know their boats and the coast well. In winter we used snowmobiles. It takes an hour and a half each way either by boat or by snowmobile. There is no airstrip in the satellite community, but a helicopter can land in the community.

We found the lady in unbearable pains and she could hardly sit up. After my initial assessment, I realised that she had a great possibility of a bleeding spleen. She did faint at one stage. Consulting the doctor on call, who suspected the same from my report, gave me the approval to arrange a medevac. We had to get her out of her community to the community I was working out of, where there was an airstrip, for a medevac plane to land. We needed a helicopter to take her there. There was a helicopter in the next community ferrying some outliers. I contacted the helicopter pilot who was also from the community I was working out of. He knew all the people of all the neighbouring communities, as you would if you're a local boy. He came as soon as he could and we had the lady transferred to the medevac plane and the medevac nurse who were already waiting at the airstrip. She was on her way to the hospital. She did damage her spleen and she did have a bleed, but they kept her on bed rest and treated her conservatively. With daily ultrasounds to check for further bleedings, she did well and didn't have to get her spleen removed. She returned home after a good spell in hospital. It was such a relief to see the lady back home on her feet again.

I had a young nephew who had to have his spleen removed after a motorbike accident. He did well after his surgery.

I had been following up a young man with abdominal pains. Suspecting he had gastritis, we had sent off stool samples to determine if he did have H. Pylori, a bacterial infection of the stomach lining. We tried him on antacids in the meantime, but he had been worsening steadily and the community doctor wasn't due for a while yet. Consulting with the community doctor, he was sent out on a regular schedule flight. After assessing him in the outpatients' clinic she decided to admit him for observation.

The doctor called me the next morning and said that the night nurses have been checking on him during the night and he slept well throughout the night. I remember that I did have him overnight at the clinic once and he had kept his eyes closed but whenever I spoke to him during the night, he was well aware I was there, and he was in pain. Most of the Inuit appear to bear their pain in silence. The doctor did consult with the surgeon and a gastroscopy found a large ulcer. In fact, he did end up with partial gastrectomy soon after that. Poor chap. He looked skinny to me before surgery, and he lost more weight by the time he came home. He did come home, and it was such a relief to see him.

Some emergencies are quite fascinating. There was a young teenager, who had been fishing with his father and had been unwell for a few days. He had been vomiting with abdominal pains. The teenager was brought in by his mother on the Friday morning when we were rushed off our feet. We do have days of calm and quietness. The community doctor had been in town as well and she was finishing up seeing the last few patients and was going to dash off to get her flight back to the hospital she works at.

The young mother and her children are rarely ill and we seldom see them at the clinic. Knowing that, I realised she must be really worried about her son to bring him in without an appointment. I got him to a side room and started asking questions and examining him at the same time. I was stopped right in my tracks when I looked at his abdomen – there was a massive swelling at the right lower abdomen. I realised it looked massive because he was slim built and had a very flat belly. The doctor checked him and, of course, knew straight away what it was: an appendiceal mass. It was the first I had ever seen and will never forget it. A medevac was arranged, and the doctor went with the patient instead of her schedule flight. The young man had surgery the same day and being a healthy teenager, recovered very well and went back to the fishing grounds with his dad soon after. Such outcomes bring a warm happy feeling in me. And best of all, I saw and learnt something new.

There is nothing like discovering something new. There is so much to learn.

When a baby or toddler is ill, they can't tell us what's wrong with them They cry and have fevers and do not want to drink or eat. When there is a child or baby brought in, then while questioning the mother, I gradually start undressing the baby at the same time looking and feeling the baby or toddler from head to toe. I assess all the vital signs and weight.

This was what I did when a young mother brought me her baby, who was about ten months old, and had been crying constantly and was not feeding well. As I was examining the baby, I realised she had a swelling from just below her ear to the jaw. The baby was quite chubby. The mother hadn't noticed this and when I identified the swelling to her, she became very upset for not having noticed it before. The poor mother was in a state and the baby was in pain with a blocked parotid gland. The baby was given analgesia and was sent out as a medevac for incision. She returned home after a few days, and she had daily dressings and packing of the wound for a good many days. The baby would start crying as soon as she saw the nurse. She recovered very well though.

SAMY WILSON

Chapter 20
Pregnant? No!

A forty-something lady turned up one night with her husband, having abdominal pains. She was quite adamant that she had no troubles passing urine. In fact, she has been peeing frequently, she said. She was unable to sit calmly and kept getting off her chair. I could see she was in a right state of great distress. I checked when her last period was, and she couldn't exactly remember as she had not been taking notice. There was no fever and all other vital signs were normal. I tested her urine she provided for infection and pregnancy. She was positive for pregnancy. She didn't believe it. Her husband couldn't believe it. On palpating her abdomen, I could feel a large mass in her lower abdomen. Then I realised what her problem was and decided to catheterise her. She was not at all happy with getting it done and she insisted there was no problems with micturition. After clarifications of my suspicions, she allowed me to proceed. The couple have one girl who was in her late teens.

She couldn't lie still. So, I had to be quick with the procedure. As soon as the urine started flowing, I could see her visually relax. Both her husband and her couldn't believe that there was that amount of urine in her. The growing uterus had been trapping the bladder in the pelvis. There was instant relief for her. Then I decided to check for a fetal heartbeat. It is the best sound ever. Even though she felt about twelve weeks, the uterus being just about palpable at the symphysis pubes, I usually could get fetal heartbeat most times. They were amazed. Then the realisation that she was actually pregnant hit her and they were quite emotional about it all.

Embarrassment came into play as well. The north then still had old-fashioned ideas and they were also considering how their daughter was going to take this dramatic news of getting a sibling at her age. I was very happy myself to have been able to solve the lady's pains. With instructions to relax in a warm bath and to pee in the bath if she had any more issues and to call if she had any further problems, she went home. I would love to have been a fly on their bedroom wall that night. I did not get a call that night. The lady came for her prenatal booking as advised, a very proud woman with her daughter to hear the baby's heartbeat again.

I love it when the job is filled with such happy outcomes.

In another community another pregnant woman, starting her third trimester came in with abdominal pain. The pain was concentrated at the left upper abdomen and back. She didn't feel well at all. Assessing her, that is checking all her usual prenatal observations, nothing was sticking out. But she was feverish. Consulting the doctor on call we decided to send her out to the obstetrician to assess her. She was found to have an abscess on her kidney, not a usual disease. Thankfully it was treated, and she went on to have a normal delivery at term.

There have been a few deliveries in the north on my watch. Thankfully, they have been normal deliveries with no problems. Including delivery of one set of twins. The first baby girl was born and then all her contractions stopped by which time the medevac midwife was on the scene as well. She delivered the second twin after she was induced to have contractions. I know they have turned out to be beautiful young ladies, I see them on Facebook frequently! One of them has my name.

Another quite interesting delivery that I will never forget was in UK when I was working as a midwife. A young woman completed her milk rounds and came on to the maternity unit and stopped her milk float at the maternity entrance. She knew she was in labour and was already having the urges to push the baby out. She was wheeled straight to the delivery room where she popped her baby out. Her first baby. She was in her early twenties and had kept her pregnancy to herself and had no prenatal follow-ups and none of her family knew. Of course, then her family were notified, and they all seemed quite pleased really. I'm unsure why she didn't share her pregnancy state with her family.

Another heartwarming case was a young woman in labour with her second pregnancy. Her first daughter was about three years old. The dad brought the three-year-old in whilst the woman was in labour to breast feed the child. That was an interesting sight in the UK. I am a Hindu, born in Malaysia, and it is not unheard of to have an older child still breast feeding whilst a woman is pregnant. The young woman was from the era of the Hippie generation and this is in the late 70s. I loved seeing that; it looked so natural.

A lot has changed since I started as a midwife. It would be interesting to see all that has changed in recent years in midwifery. Motherhood and bringing up children have evolved over the years.

Chapter 21

Nurses

There was more to do as a northern nurse then being a nurse in a hospital. The best thing about being a northern nurse is being able to learn to cope with all the different roles. To be able to learn from one another and not be dogmatic. I learnt not to be after a while. Working in isolation, we learnt to get along with one another. For some, it takes a while to adjust to the new role. In my opinion, a successful and soul-satisfying northern nurse is only achieved by working together.

Over the years from 1972 to 2020, I have had the opportunity to work with an amazing number of health professionals. Nurses and midwives were the biggest influence in my professional life. It goes without saying that I gained my experiences working with some of the best of them.

I have met some wonderful nurses. Caring, kind-hearted and compassionate ones. I have met some who were just there doing the basics. They are the ones who simply do not have the patience and tolerance for the sick. I have often wondered why they ever entered the nursing profession. Then there are the ones who, as young children, had been sick in hospital and have had good, loving care from nurses and so they become nurses. One of the male nurses in my diploma training was one of those.

Another male nurse went into nursing because his mother was a nurse. But if you asked my nephew, Mariano, why he chose nursing, he would tell you that his mother, that's my sister, took him to the nursing school to enrol him and he didn't have a choice. He just didn't have any other career options in mind either. It worked out for the best for my nephew. He loves what he does now and he works in Singapore with his nurse-wife, Vetha.

I have two sisters, Ambigai and Yoges, who are nurses. They love what they do. They worked hard to achieve their ambitions to be where they are: two successful young women. There are a few family members who are nurses too. Two of my nephews' wives are nurses and I know they love what they do. A nephew and a niece are nurses as well. I loved nursing but funnily enough, it wasn't something I dreamt of doing as a career option – like my nephew Mariano. Some of my closest friends are undoubtedly nurses, people I have worked with over the years. We may not be in touch for a few years then for some reason or other when we do talk, it's like picking up where we left off.

During my training as a Diploma nurse, I didn't want to administer my first intramuscular injection. I didn't want to push a needle into anyone's body part. A curmudgeon of a Ward Sister knew I didn't want to do it. She took me to a comatose lady and pulled the bed curtain around and stood over me and told me where and how to do it. I stood frozen by that bedside. She actually cupped her hands over mine to give the lady her injection. I don't remember what that injection was and why I was giving it to her. But I did it. It was plain sailing after that I must admit. I will never forget that Ward Sister. She was very tall and skinny, never smiled, but I remember her as a kind person. She never scolded or shouted at a nurse. She had the nurses doing what needed to be done efficiently.

As a student nurse, I was trailing a staff nurse in a urology ward. She was a young, beautiful blonde with a heart of gold. She was aware of my great trepidation of dying patients. As a Hindu, we carry out numerous rituals for the dead. Not doing those rituals didn't seem right to me. I suppose being straight out of the east and being pretty ignorant of the rest of the world, helped in my narrow-minded thinking. One day she took me to the bedside of a dying patient, who was not to be resuscitated. We sat with her, and the staff nurse held the patient's hand until she died. She showed me how to wash a dead person and lay her out for her family to view her. She was so gentle with her and she taught me such a valuable lesson that day. She taught me how to be comfortable with a dying patient. Through the years when I sat with a dying patient, I always remembered that nurse. That valuable lesson has also helped me help families to be with their loved ones during the hard final moments.

An incident I remember so clearly to this day was of an elderly gentleman who had shown up with abdominal pains. It was a weekend. The nurse on call (NOC), did not respond to the doorbell straight away. I knew this because living in the clinic residence I got to know all the sounds including sounds of vehicles stopping at the clinic. I didn't hear the clinic door opening so I came down to see this elder crouched on the floor at the door holding his abdomen. He did not make any sound and his daughter was standing next to him. I opened the clinic door to let him in and straight to the emergency bed. Then the nurse on call saunters in. The daughter had phoned first before coming to the clinic. I left them with the nurse and returned to my apartment.

Not soon after, most probably ten to fifteen minutes maximum, I heard the door and saw the elder and his daughter being picked up. I saw him struggling to get into the truck. I knew he should not have been sent home even though I had only seen him for a few short minutes. At least he should have been observed in the clinic for at least an hour. But I didn't examine him. I was still worried though. Not many minutes passed, maybe another fifteen minutes, I heard a truck stop at the clinic, buzzed for the nurse on call and a man leaving with the stretcher.

There was no doubt in my mind who that stretcher was for, and I was not satisfied that the right things were being done for the patient and decided to speak to the nurse in charge.

I was not going to wait for a bad outcome. There had been a few complaints already regarding the nurse's attitude towards patients and many had already refused to see her. In a small community people talk and rumours spread like wildfire. I informed the Nurse-in-Charge (NIC) of my concerns. We went down to see what's going on and at the same time the patient was being carried in on the stretcher.

Rightly so, the nurse on call became defensive straight away. She went on to say she had checked him out and had also consulted with the doctor on call and on the doctor's advice had sent the patient home with analgesia. I didn't say anything and the NIC was polite and listened to the NOC calmly and said we will help as well.

Assessing him I realised he had reduced bowel sounds and he had an acute abdomen. The NIC called the doctor on call and submitted our findings, and the doctor, of course, was surprised at our findings when she had a different report just a little earlier, that in no way suggested any urgency. He was medevacked out and returned home after a while with a colostomy. It does make me shudder to think of what could have happened.

I don't think that nurse ever returned to the north. The north has a very small population and you get to hear everything. Especially who is stationed where.

Numerous times I have seen nurses make light of a patient's complaint. Especially when they are brought to the clinic as an emergency. There is no sense of empathy by the nurse dealing with a patient who appears to be in an acute state. Either because they may not have taken enough pills for a proper suicide attempt, or they have inflicted a small stab wound to their body or a gunshot wound just enough to wound themselves. I have seen all these and more of nurses speaking aloud and belittling their attempt. It is a sad fact that some nurses have absolutely no patience and no kindness in them.

Then there are the nurses who simply are kind and gentle with the above patients. I have been privileged and honoured to have worked with more good nurses than the not so good. There are more good nurses but the bad few bring down the profession's integrity. Like the case of the UK nurse, Lucy Letby, who was convicted of killing babies in August 2023. That's over the top I know, but it smears the profession. People wonder who to trust if not the nurse or the doctor.

I worked with one of the most charming, French-Canadian nurses. She was, wholeheartedly a people person – simply the best. She would go out of her way to help people, especially young teenagers. One of the things she did promote enthusiastically was birth control to prevent teenage pregnancy. Teenage pregnancy was not addressed candidly at that time. She would take time to talk to the youth about contraception; any time, any place. She was well respected and well liked in the communities she worked in.

Sadly, there are some nurses with addiction problems. I personally only knew of one with addiction to a control drug. She would help herself to some and doctor the file to place a patient's name. It was not identified soon enough. She did leave the profession. She was a very lovable person. I was sad to know how she left.

Another young woman drank alcohol, even on duty. She was put on sick leave and had counselling. She appeared to have mastered her demon. I hope she did.

Colleagues of mine have had to deal with nurses with addictions and it's their stories to tell. I just want to say that there are nurses who need help too.

SAMY WILSON

Chapter 22

She Walks the Corridor

Very often as a nurse in a community you are told there is "someone" walking the corridors at night. Almost all the clinics I have been to, have a story.

One near middle of the night, a man was wanting some strong analgesia for chronic pains. He has regular prescription for opioids, but he takes more than he should and runs out. It was a challenge to manage him. It was also difficult to refuse him knowing he does have genuine pains as MRI revealed the cause of his pains.

After giving him his pills and, as he was leaving, he looked up the corridor and said, "Oh, she is still around then." On questioning him, he proceeded to tell me that a young girl with long hair is always seen walking the corridors at night. Usually from her back. I was not impressed. So, I told him to wait, and I walked up the corridor and checked the rooms leading off the corridor and didn't see anyone and I told him that there was no-one. He went home and I locked up and went back to my apartment.

In another community, a nurse told me she often sees a young girl in the clinic at nights. The nurse is a good friend of mine.

Another nurse in another clinic told me that a young girl will follow her round in the clinic at night, when she has to be up for emergencies and will follow her up the stairs but, at the door to her apartment, my friend tells her to stop and that she can't come any further. It's always a little girl. So, the nurses are smart and intelligent people. So, what are they seeing that I can't? Or is it that not everyone is privileged to be able to see what others do?

When I was a midwife in the UK and before my time, I remember the midwives telling me of a young mother dying after giving birth to her baby. They talked of a dove appearing and staying around until the baby was discharged and only then did the dove fly away. Is there anything to these tales? I have no idea. It is comforting though to think that the mother who died still kept an eye on her baby.

Conclusion

"You're so vain! You probably think this song is about you," by Carly Simon, kept playing in my mind whilst I was writing this book. I don't know why. Or maybe I know why. Maybe, I have to remind myself that writing a memoir and thinking that anyone would be interested might be vanity!

There was plenty more to write about. How much is too much? Will all that I have narrated bore some to death? I have left a lot out for other reasons: a child drowning, rapes, unwanted babies, SIDS and emotionally charged cases that I felt unable to broach. I have laid them to rest.

Nursing has given me, in many ways, a good life. I have met so many people along the way and most of them are people who I call friends. During our times working together we might have had differences. It's like being married. You have differences with the man in your life. You love the man. So, I have great love for the many friendships I have made over the years. I have come away with peace and contentment and a feeling of having given my best. Having said that, It doesn't mean that ever so often, I don't have twinges that I could have done some things differently. It's human frailties.

Nursing has allowed me to be financially Independent. Besides, being able to help my own family in various ways has been a blessing.

My outlook on life has broadened and blossomed. I came into nursing with very narrow-minded ideas and views being fresh out of a village in Malaysia. Even though I was an avid reader from childhood, I must have compartmentalised what I have read as fiction. Rightly so, I suppose. Many things I saw and learnt in nursing had to be processed in my mind and threshed out to view things in its proper context. Bryan, my husband was instrumental in helping me thresh them out like hay: separating the chaff from the wheat. He has the patience of a saint to have put up with me all these years and to have let me travel away from him to the distant land. He trusted me to do the right and honourable things. I am ever grateful to him.

My siblings and my mother, my nieces and nephews (my father died young, but he was proud of me), were interested in my nursing and my travels. My writing a memoir is for them, too. I am looking forward to hearing from my colleagues and nurses in general what they think of this book. I am gearing myself for whatever is going to be thrown at me.

Author Biography

Samy Wilson, née Precalavathy Sinnasamy, is a Tamil in Malaysia, educated at St. Marguerite's Convent in Bukit Mertajam, Penang. She studied nursing at Joyce Green Hospital, Dartford, Kent, and later at Burnley, Lancashire, for specialisation in midwifery. She married a Lancashire lad, called Bryan.

With a career that spanned over a decade in the United Kingdom, Samy devoted herself to nursing and midwifery. This was followed by a remarkable thirty-five year tenure as a northern nurse in Canada.

Her personal narrative is coloured by global travels, seamlessly bridging distances between Malaysia and Canada to nurture family ties, and between Cyprus and Canada in her professional capacity. In the end, Samy selected the idyllic island of Cyprus with her husband as her sanctuary for retirement.

SAMY WILSON

Printed in Poland
by Amazon Fulfillment
Poland Sp. z o.o., Wrocław